STRAIGHT AROUND ALLEN

On the Business of Being Allen Ginsberg

for philip + Kyle

by Bob Rosenthal

*good friends
and bearers of the
light!*

BobRosenthal
12/19/18   NYC

Published by Beatdom Books

View the publisher's website:
www.books.beatdom.com

Printed in the United Kingdom

First Print Edition
ISBN 978-0-9934099-4-3

Table Of Contents

1 Theory of Idiots

once to the heart I am filled by
light that can't switch off
a ball rolls off finger tips
pizza dough rises from the palm
a rocket melts the launching tower
a car parallel parks in two moves
men with rubber hoses enter the room
light is still here
even to the landlord who has no name
no hot water no heat

———

I am a lonely child who likes adventures. In Junior High School, I read *Moby Dick* for the action. I read the whole book and only recall the excitement of the chase. As it turns out, I re-read *The Whale*'s life opus every ten years. At college, I am taught that the non-fiction about whales and whaling heighten the drama between Ahab and Starbuck. As I read the novel again and again, Ishmael's meditations move me most.

Call me Bob. I walk down Linden Avenue to the Baiha'i Temple near my childhood home. I gaze into the latticed dome of my future shapeless illumination.

1977 NEW YORK CITY – Sunlight beats through the high-boxed windows on the east kitchen wall. Asher Levy public school is not visible through the sun-drenched street windows. The coffee steams in my hand. I'm happy. I am newly laid off from the Lone Star Café. I will receive unemployment for at least six months. Time is mine to spend as I wish. I am a real poet at last! Shelley is a glowing love-buddy immersed in the first big rush of pregnancy. I realize that this is the moment I've been waiting for. I am on Easy Street! I walk from the sink to the kitchen table. The phone rings. Easy Street is over.

Memory is never a straight line. Memories flood the imagination like the tide coming in. One cannot fight it.

One cannot hold a flood in one's hands. How are stories distilled from the vastness of experience? The keys are episodic emotionally and rationally; these may be contradictory. Nonfiction subject headings flood the course; sailing into the stiff wind of Allen Ginsberg, I tack my way forward. Poesies appear as masthead outlooks.

Ted is both friend and mentor. I read the Beat writers but I love the New York School poets. If James Schuyler calls, I'll faint.

On September 27, 1977, I walk from East 11th Street to East 12th Street to meet Allen.

Before embarking, I have to give a small sermon on what motivates writers: Money? Fame? Sex? Or is it an obsession that will not be otherwise assuaged? I try to write about Ginsberg for years without success. It depresses me and forces me to leave the Ginsberg world's employ. I have to get beyond the surf and the barrier islands to open veins of electronic ink. Ginsberg is a natural topic. Ego demands its lubrication. There has to be more to writing. I am beginning without the knowledge of accomplishment. Moby Dick cannot be killed. In an age of selfies, I am obsessed. I have to struggle with Allen along with my devotions. A good conflict makes holiness believable. My own poetry is included to be absolutely embarrassing. Allen didn't see or approve or promote this poetry. Allen's influences are an invisible education. The sea gaze is changeable like a sudden squall on the horizon.

"It's Allen Ginsberg here!" I am surprised but not shocked. I've met Allen a few times. We were neighbors on East 12th Street. He explains that his regular secretary Richard Elovich is in Europe. Richard wants to stay longer. Allen calls Ted Berrigan to recommend a substitute. Ted recommends me.

Allen coyly asks if I would like to work with him for a little while. Ted tells me later that his only concern is whether I could "put up with" Allen. Not the other way around. I see my unemployment checks disappearing as I hear myself say "Yes of course!" He asks me how much free time I have? I mention that Shelley is pregnant.

"When is she due?"

"April."

"Oh that's ok. There'll be plenty of time."

I wonder what he means.

He tells me to come over the next day. I walk back to the building I had skipped out of the year before. Allen and Peter Orlovsky are out front on the street. Allen is wearing a tweed coat and cap. He has a bright Indian shoulder bag embedded with little mirrors dangling by his side. I am as nervous as anyone would be starting a new job. I am not stepping out of my world. Indeed I am stepping into it

Allen greets me in a grave manner. He says Con Edison is threatening to turn off his power. He hands me the turn-off notice and a check for $46.79. Allen asks me to go to Con Ed and pay it. I march to Union Square. Wait in line on the first floor of the Con Edison Building. I hand the lady the turn-off notice and the check. I wait for the receipt. I rush back to East 12th Street. Allen is upstairs. Having been instructed to yell up I holler

"AAALLEN!" His head pops out of the center window. He waves to me. His head disappears into the apartment for a moment. Allen re-emerges with a dark object. He quickly tosses it out the window. A hapless woolen sock that has lost its mate holds a set of keys. It bounces on the cement sidewalk before me. I let myself in. Climb the three flights to apartment number twenty-three. The door is slightly ajar. I step inside and stand for a moment. I am facing a long hallway whose end is sun-filled.

I hand Allen the receipt. He seems favorably impressed. Is he so easy to please? I wonder. We talk about my work schedule. He needs me for several hours a day. I am now in the service of Allen Ginsberg. I know that I will remain a poet. I do not realize I will have to hide my poems and dissolve my personal ambition.

In W.B. Yeats's *A Vision* I am a phase four of the moon. In Yeats's schema for the fourth phase the beginnings of ambition are present. Their attainment is not. I am primary in focus not secondary. I seem to have a kind of wisdom that is practical not abstract. Yeats describes "a wisdom of saws and proverbs." Allen Ginsberg with his prodigious intelligence and vast memory of verses seems to need a deliberate fellow to follow him like a tiger's tail that extends and bends to create balance. I am the phase to be that fellow.

Chicago Imagination: Big Shoulders

Born in Chicago. I am a child in the suburbs. The orange streetlamps glow over the city horizon. Beckon me to find the blues to find poetry to find love. I am an introvert. I often fail to make a good first impression. I read Moby Dick in my 13th year. A pretty good fish story. I am Ishmael looking for Ahab and a white whale.

1950 is the year of the Tiger. I am birthed in Leo's sun. Harry Truman is the president. My birth is lost in the dog days of summer. A Hebrew Calendar looksee at my birth reveals the most wonderful month: the moon of Elul. The ram's horn is blown in the morning prayer service to wake up sleeping souls and prepare them for the self examination that comes in the Moon of Tishrei, but I am born on the fourth day of Elul and self realization is a long way off. I know that I will never be the youngest anything.

Here is the homeport in my voyage to boil down the oil of Ginsberg and light lamps against the darkness that always is coming.

I set out into the woods each day without meaning to. I sit. Around the time of my twenty-first birthday I realize that my life's occupation is writing poetry. My college poet friend Steve Toth and his wife Sheila are visiting Shelley and me in Northern Wisconsin. We carouse with ditch weed and Jose Cuervo. We stagger out of the Namakagon Chief into a night sky flowing bilious ribbons of Northern Lights. The next day they drive off. I experience two weeks of rudimentary spiritual awakening. I start with morning coffee sloshing over fingers to sit in the forest. Sunshine. Shadows. Sunshine. After ten days I stay inside the cottage. Bang out a poem on my mother's black manual Remington. For the first time I write a poem that works on multiple levels. Uses a consistent conceit. It ends "I will leave my rusty cabbage by the lake." I accept the mantle of poet.

Becoming a poet allows me to avoid adopting a career.

I seek out poets at the crowded urban campus of the University of Illinois Chicago Circle. The Vietnam War is channeling all men into college hoping to escape the war by studying. I find a group of poets who conduct an alternative poetry workshop. We take turns reading poems and receiving criticism. The comments are constructive. Honest observations are invaluable to budding writers. Friends tell me that New York poet Ted Berrigan is teaching at nearby Northeastern Illinois University. A few of us sit in on his classes. He introduces the idea of living in New York City to write poems. Ted recommends we subscribe to the mimeo magazine *The World* published by the Poetry Project.

Ted is printing Alice Notley's mimeo poetry magazine *Chicago*. I get to know Ted because I own a dark green VW Squareback. I help Ted move the boxes of paper on a hot day. He stands sweating in his skivvies. Teaches me how to run a mimeo machine.

Poetry is my entire life in Chicago. Shelley starts to write poems. My Circle Campus coeditors consist of Richard Friedman. Peter Kostakis. Darlene Pearlstein. Don Nisonoff. We start *The Milk Quarterly* and discover other groups of Chicago poets. The *Stone Wind* gang are Hank Kanabus. Terry Jacobus. Al Simmons. John Paul. The *Oink* magazine crew Paul Hoover. James Leonard. Dean Faulwell.

Ted's wife Alice Notley shows up one evening at his workshop. She is unmistakably pregnant. Tips back a bottle of Gallo Burgundy. I am prudishly horrified at this Dickensian vision of dissipation. Shelley and I soon know Alice and Ted better. They both encourage us to move to New York City. We check Gotham out by driving Ted to a poetry reading there. Ted reads his journal poem *Train Ride* in a loft on Greene Street. Shelley and I stay with Dick and Carol Gallup on East 4th Street and Avenue B. 1972 it is a veritable badlands. Garish high-intensity street lamps cast sharp shadows. Perpetual siren screams and stinking garbage in the streets do not deter us. I propose marriage and New York City to Shelley. A poet's promise of no career and no money. For some reason Shelley accepts.

We move to New York City in September 1973. Sell the car and book a compartment on Amtrak's Lake Shore Ltd. We slowly pull out of Chicago seeking the poetry community existing within the *World Magazine*. It is very hot. The air-conditioning doesn't work. We sweat in our underwear. Look at each other with trepidation. The train brings us into Grand Central Station at daybreak.

Ted tells us to stay at the Hotel Chelsea. Manhattan yellows in the heat. We walk around

----

I think that I can always be a poet even if I have to sell pencils on the street. However, I am wrong; no one on the street begs with pencils any more.

Alice feeds me my first okra.

I tell Shelley that we don't have to stay but we both are already smitten and know there is no way back.

———

I am a Manhattanized chameleon; absorbing avenues of brightness and unforgiving dark pavements. I blink at the corner of 7th Avenue and 23rd Street. It is hard to take my eyes off it.

———

We swap our real mothers and fathers for the poetic arms of our new mama, the Lower East Side.

———

This arrangement well suits Allen's synchronistic but partitioned personal personae.

———

Allen loves this rabbit warren of rooms. He shoots a movie, *Household Affairs,* that examines the entire scene.

———

Although Allen's sense of privacy extends to very few places, one place is the tub. The bath sheds gross reality and reveals the purest nudity; the tub is a metaphor always ready to serve.

a little. Go back to our room. Disturb the cockroaches. Water starts to cascade through the bathroom ceiling. I run down to inform the clerk at the desk. He looks up at me. Sarcastically says "It must be the beginning of the end of the world." I go back to our room. Tell Shelley that we could always go home. But we don't leave. We understand from novels that we should either live on the Upper West Side or the Lower East Side. We have no criteria by which to choose between these two neighborhoods. When we ascend the Empire State Building the Upper West Side sky is gray and dark with rainclouds about to break open. The Lower East Side is sunny and clear with blue sky. So we decide to go Lower East to start a new home.

It is strange to come back to a building from which I recently fled. I fear the hideous landlady and her looks of remonstrance. I walk by her on the apartment stairs a few times without hearing Polish abuse. I relax. Endure her quiet glare.

The two apartments have long been conjoined. But they always feel like different apartments. Apartment twenty-two opens onto the large rhomboid kitchen with built-in brown cabinets. A long wooden counter. A square metal table. There are two bedrooms. A water-closet. The north-facing windowsill over the radiator holds dozens of copies of the New York Times.

Down the long hallway straight ahead is the T-shaped apartment twenty-three. The office and Allen's bedroom with their south-facing windows sit opposite the green cornice of Mary Help of Christians Church. Allen's bedroom has a large hand-made captain's bed. Bookcases. Buddhist shrine. Meditation pads. Small desk. The second bedroom is converted into a room holding a bathtub and linen storage cabinet. This is divided from a narrow three-sided galley library lined with brown bookcases. They overflow with books. Of the six windows that punctuate the apartment there is one at the bathtub. A solitary sunny tub on heavily painted feet. The area is visually cut off if the linen cabinet door is open. A necessity for a shy Buddhist.

Can one discuss a body without listening to the heart? The office is Allen's heart; it is the seat of both his passion and his intelligence. The entire flat throbs to its beat.

Allen feels safe inside of a miasma that he creates. There are parallel universes for his loved ones to inhabit. He is the epicenter of each; he leaves in order to return with fresh winds, as fresh as the wild apples, and the dirt in Peter's mane. Allen breathes unfettered only by caring for all humanity. He leads five lifetimes in one, not five consecutive lives.

Allen's office is completely lined with old pale green or brown filing cabinets. It is first-hand knowledge stored in second-hand drawers. A long dark piece of plywood supported by two sets of filing cabinets serves as a desk big enough for two people to work side by side. An empty peanut butter jar holds pens and pencils. A larger jar for rulers letter openers large markers. They rest side by side on the desk. There is a pale blue manual Smith-Corona portable typewriter that had belonged to Allen's father. A jumble of posters and papers are jammed between the desk and the wall. Large manila envelopes boldly labeled **Ordinary Mail** or **Business Mail** or **Literary Letters** are stacked at one end of the desk. A brown paper shopping bag under the desk is labeled **Junk Mail**. A large black marbled notebook lies open by the telephone to collect innumerable messages. The filing cabinets supporting the desk contain personal files. Allen's will and medical records are in the top (fullest) drawer. A sticker on it reads **Death and Asshole**. Another drawer contains business records such as publishing contracts for books and recordings. In the corner there are three full-sized banged up filing cabinets. Each drawer is labeled in Allen's handwriting. **Dope. Dope. Dope. Mostly Dope. FBI COINTELPRO. FBI Cream.**

My primary responsibility is to fetch the mail from the postbox at Stuyvesant Station. Open and sort the letters for Allen. Answer any mail that Allen specifies. At first I work three or four hours a day. I come over in the mid-afternoon and work until the early evening. By my dinnertime Allen is primed. Eager to work more.

The East 12th Street apartment is always pulsating with

action. Denise is forming a punk rock band called *Stimulators*. Her mates come over to practice. I am typing responses to the mail. Updating Allen's month-by-month date book. Four or five cassette tapes arrive in the mail. They must be processed and indexed. Allen cares about the index exceedingly. He enjoys using it himself.

Peter bursts into the city in coveralls. His long graying hair falls behind his energetic frame. He brings wild apples and vegetables in his shabby blue Volvo wagon. He is always sweet to me. He calls me "Bobby." I don't mind. He serves me cups of coffee at my desk and is always courteous.

Allen groggily arises in a white sleeveless t-shirt and briefs. Allen has many visitors and overnight guests. There are coat hooks for towels by the bathtub with names painted beneath. The refrigerator is usually well stocked. Guests are free to eat without asking permission. But are also expected to refill the larder. I discover that I have to make that clear to guests.

This is Allen's way of making a home. It is fundamentally communist from aesthetics to practice. The chaotic atmosphere of people wandering in and out through the rooms pleases me. It allows me to see my world completely contextualized. I realize that I can multitask. I give in to the overall energy in the Ginsberg home. I start to discover what the routines are. I type a letter. Answer the phone. Run to the window to toss the key sock down. Run back to the desk. Continue the sentence. Allen is pleased with me. He is slow to build up my workload.

Peter Orlovsky has a bedroom; ample sized and sunlit. Denise Mercedes, Peter's lover, lives in this room as Peter spends most of his time on East Hill on the Committee on Poetry farm.

There are some enterprises in which a careful disorderliness is the true method. Melville, from *Moby Dick*

Allen is Queequeg to my Ishmael. I fear his untamed nature and take solace in his certainty of both worldly skill and deep spiritual connection. I creep into his bed for years to come and love him as a member of my family, making me a man and father too.

I am waking to the real power of being awake

The Theory

Allen has a job for everybody. He is a creator of work. The first lesson I learn is the Theory of Idiots. I discover the theory after I manage to annoy many people. Allen wants a new pro-bono lawyer to receive a photocopy of a case file that only one friend is in possession of. He instructs me to call three other people who also know this one fellow. Ask each one of them to tell the document holder to send a copy of the file to the new lawyer. Naturally I am to call the document holder directly. I call the three people. Next call the holder of the documents myself. He complains bitterly that at least two others have called to tell him the same thing. He sends the copy.

I ask Allen why he has me ask three people to do the same thing. Allen tells me. "It's the 'Theory of Idiots!' It goes like this. You are an idiot. She over there is an idiot. He in the next room taking a bath is an idiot. And I am an idiot." I still have a puzzled expression on my face. "You see. You ask every idiot to do the same thing. Then one of them might actually do it!" Ah! I see the light. The Theory of Idiots works. The cost is redundancy and annoyance. As I gain experience I form my own assessment. Who will do as one requests? Who needs extra prodding? I labor under and then master the Theory of Idiots. I become smart enough to avoid tongue-lashings from fellow idiots. The idiot's bottom line is "get it done!"

I count myself lucky when Denise Mercedes practices in the kitchen with the fledgling *Stimulators*. Anne Gustavsson's bass and Denise's electric guitar are not amped. The apartment lacks air-conditioning. Denise and Anne are playing at the kitchen table in their underwear. Often they work long and hard to come up with novel chord progressions. Quiet metallic chords are heard with occasional whoops of joy when a good riff is found. Their concentration is remarkable. It takes most of my concentration not to stare at them sitting over splayed legs sweating above their guitars. Denise and I get along fine. We keep out of each other's way. Find ways to be helpful to each other. I help Harley Flanagan (Denise's nephew and *Stimulators* drummer) with his seventh grade math homework. At Denise's request I call a local radio station after they play their single *Loud Fast Rules.* Request it again.

Allen grabs all of my attention by giving me a daunting task. He has been spending the last several years in Boulder teaching at the Naropa Institute. He sends two large boxes of archival materials to New York. The cartons contain notebooks. Manila envelopes filled with mail. Manuscripts in clip binders. Cassette tape recordings. Business papers. The post office doesn't deliver the boxes. Later the PO informs us that the boxes have been lost in a train wreck. I spend months trying to recover any part of the shipment. To no avail. I become aware of how deep Allen's obsession with saving everything goes. These are among the first items from his archives that were ever legitimately lost (not stolen by "friends").

Allen is told by Columbia University's Butler Library to save all of his work. Send it over to be held on deposit. Allen retains ownership and controls access to the papers. Butler has the right of first refusal for any sales.

I am snowed under by Allen's huge correspondence. Three inches of letters accumulate at Stuyvesant Station every day. I slice them all. Allen tells me not to open the most personal ones. Those are limited to Edith his stepmother and Eugene his brother. It gives me a perverse pleasure to see a poet's letter addressed to Allen with **Personal – Allen Only** boldly printed on it. I eagerly insert the red Chinese dragon letter opener. The letters are first sorted into categories. **Literary** letters from friends. **Business** correspondence from publishers. Agents and universities seeking an appearance. **Ordinary** brochures. Newsletters. Fan mail. Lastly **Junk** mail. I flatten the letters out and sort them. I prioritize each pile for interest or urgency. Allen will get to them late at night.

I arrive in the afternoon. I find his scribbled responses to the

_____
Our diligence pays off when a few tattered notebooks are returned.

———

Most likely, he will answer them at night or just before dawn.

———

I notice that Allen likes to dive to the bottom of the priority pile; start with the least important. These interest him most. Letters often arrive which are several pages long, densely handwritten on both sides in a tiny, cramped hand. I try to read the written convolutions but get dizzy and stop. Allen devours the whole letter and reorders the ideas by numbering them to make sense of it. He walks me through the letter, proud of his ability to understand the thought progressions. "Any reply?" I ask, impressed! "Oh no!" Allen laughs, "He would only write a longer letter!"

———

In every Russian soul, there is the fool that sings for Mother Russia. That song always holds Allen in its sway.

Doesn't this extreme openness indicate an even larger reserve of unclutteredness? Allen's annoying theory that everyone is an idiot is true just as it is also true that no one is an idiot.

———

I wonder if Allen makes up the idiotic theory just this once to answer my idiotic question. Or, does it stem from a routine he and William joke about on East 7th Street in 1953? Either way, it is the way the world spins. Eyes wide open and heart on the table!

———

Jack Kerouac describes Allen as a pushy, in-your-face angry creature, but that is not the Allen I first meet.

previous day's mail. Sometimes a letter requires a response. Often I need to take a short walk to the copy shop to make copies to send out to others. I prepare new letters on the manual typewriter. I try to make the letters simple and clear. Allen copyedits the letter. Decides if retyping is necessary. He adds hand-inked comments at the bottom.

Allen has special skill in deciphering the most confused and anguished letters. To Allen mental pain is a means of expressing love. The pain in these convoluted letters excites him by bringing him back to a primal love.

Allen is a close reader of legal texts. He ably analyzes the terms of a legal contract. He teaches me how contractual permissions or releases try to steal ownership of one's own work and biography. Permissions never go out without many initialed cross-outs.

The Theory of Idiots leads me to become less of an idiot myself. It's a loaded word. I soon realize from Allen's library that he is well schooled in Russian literature. Dostoyevsky's *The Idiot* is one of his favorite novels. Prince Myshkin is delightfully honest and open. With the best of intentions shatters the life of every other character. Allen's highly private openness and naïveté create a disarming charm. Like Myskin he is hard to ignore.

I begin to understand the individuals in this new solar system. In the Ginsberg universe Allen is a sun with many people orbiting him. It seems as if there is free will. But the gravitational pull of Allen is what drives our paths now.

It takes years to learn most of all the person Allen is. He loves to get into heated political discussions on the phone at least once every two weeks. He hones his frightening moral authority.

He seems relaxed, calm, and patient. Yes, occasionally, he flares up over a trifle such as the placement of his pencils. It isn't until years later that I hear old tapes of Allen being pushy and even rude. I figure Buddhist meditation has mollified his angry frame of mind.

He needs me to answer the phone but he hovers nearby when it rings.

Deeply explores his argumentative reserves. When he hangs up he emits a sigh of satisfaction. He releases a lot of built-up tension.

Allen only shows me generosity. I try to be neutral to the person on the phone. They demand to speak with Allen "right away." I find out their name. I reply "I am not sure if Allen is around but I will try to find him." I cover the mouth of the telephone receiver to ask Allen if he wants to talk to this person. When he does. I make Allen wait a few more seconds. As if he is coming through the room to answer. Allen tells me he likes my style. I don't tell a lie yet I give no information away.

2 Lower East Side: Wetlands

from *To My Baby Spoon & Fork*

Did Pieter Stuyvesant hear a distant rumble as he skated over 1st Avenue?
Did he hear a cry of Tuinal and Elavil on wide pear tree-lined 14th Street
And now where Neil lives perhaps there was once a picket fence
Now Stuyvesant High School conducts laboratory tests
Where a creek used to flow like the IRT through Stuyvesant's dream
The sun rose in full view without being blocked by Stuyvesant Town
Or Tania Towers or Con Ed blasting its white acrid smoke

This window is my desk on East 11th Street; it seems to catalog a changing neighborhood and welcome the city becoming.

———

There is no connected automation to do the work; I am all-in-one.

I BECOME LESS OF AN IDIOT in the Ginsberg dominion. The tellers in the post office become acquainted with me. They get our mail ready as soon as they see me get in line. I visit the copy shop often. Know everyone there. Allen keeps multiple copies of many seminal papers to send out as needed. In the 1970s it takes a big effort to mail copies. It means a short trek to 1st Avenue to buy the copies. Hike back to the apartment to collate. Staple. Fill the envelopes. Seal them. Stuff into a shopping bag. Walk back outside. Head to the Post Office. Wait in line with petty cash in hand.

Managing Allen's time is one of my daily tasks. Allen keeps his planner in his cloth Indian shoulder bag. I pull it out. Make changes to it. We use pencil. Allen is the holder of the plan. His poetry readings are arranged by agent Charles Rothschild who Allen meets through Albert Grossman (Dylan's agent). Charlie is a burly voice on the phone. One can hear his large moustache brushing the handset as he speaks. I keep in touch with Charlie's office all the time to keep Allen's schedule current. Charlie makes a date. I check the date in Allen's planner. I make sure that Charlie sends out the proper instructions for the stage set-up. I do as much work as Charlie does to manage each gig. This extra effort is necessary because Allen values his poetry readings. He is rejuvenated by the flow of energy when he reads his poems to an attentive audience. He always gives 100% of his attention to a poetry reading.

Although Allen travels constantly he adores the Lower East Side's cheap diners and ethnic flavors. His 12th Street front door is located where few people are willing to venture. His apartments are dumps. The fixtures and walls are from 1900. The windows heavy and misshapen. The rent is cheap. In bed Allen reads the *Times*. Scribbles down poems. Makes prosaic entries in his journals. He falls asleep just before Mr. Boungiorno (next door neighbor) leaves his door. Walks across the street to ring the 6AM bells at Mary Help of Christians Church. To the Lower East Side Allen is a local celebrity. People wave and say "Hi." Everyone knows who he is. LES denizens feel a little ownership that he chooses to live among them.

———
Managing Allen is a piece of cake; all Charlie has to do is answer the phone and open the mail.

———
The set-up is simple but detailed. It calls for a particular kind of music stand, Manhasset, and a particular kind of chair, kitchen. How many hours do I have to spend talking about what a flat-bottomed chair is and is not?

———
A university in Japan goes so far as to build the chair. I carefully measure one of Allen's kitchen chairs and they re-create it. It remains in their library, lovingly called the Allen Ginsberg chair.

———
Lower East Side provides safe conduct from Moloch.

Emerging in New York

Soon we had our first cool New York City apartment.

———

Five Rules For LES Street Smarts:

1. Always look like you know where you are going.

2. Be aware of people behind you without turning to look.

3. Have your door key cupped in your hand ready to insert in the street door lock or gouge into an assailant's face.

4. Separate your cash. Leave a few bucks in your wallet but hide the rest elsewhere (not your shoe).

5. (Advanced) Mula bandha creates an aura that allows you to walk through groups of scary people without them seeing you.

———

Creeley is my first courage giver in poetry. In a poetry course U. of Iowa, I have to buy a book of poems from a list. Creeley's *For Love* has the most poems for the lowest price. The violence of the complex short poems baffles me. But, during a short breakup with Shelley in Chicago, the poems leap off the page and show me what truth really looks like!

———

There is an ever present group of young Puerto Rican men who control the street and strip stolen cars.

———

Shelley is working as a secretary at the Poetry Project and I am going to graduate school at CCNY and cleaning houses.

Down from the Empire State Building Shelley and I look in the *Times* real estate section. Find a Lower East Side listing on St. Marks Place. It is up three flights of stairs at the back. It has ladder and sleeping loft. Ailanthus leaves can be seen through the windows. This is our new worldview. We do not really know where in the city we are. Through the leaves I notice a weather vane atop a church steeple. I wonder where St. Mark's Church is. I know there is poetry to be found there. I don't realize that I am actually looking at St. Mark's weathervane. The quiet and quaint nature of St. Mark's Place and 2nd Avenue in 1973 is just a breather post-freak and pre-punk!

Shelley and I meet poets at the St. Marks Poetry Project. One of them is an older gentleman Larry Fagin. After a reading he invites Shelley and me to his apartment on East 12th Street promising to show us cool mimeo poetry magazines. We accompany him down a dark miserable block. A dilapidated single story abandoned bus depot sits on the South side. Semi-abandoned apartments are facing it on the North side. Larry's building is opposite a beautiful Italianate catholic church. He shows us his rare books. Larry asks us back again after another poetry reading at the Poetry Project. We realize he likes to have company walking down East 12th Street.

Poet Rebecca Wright offers us her apartment on East 12th Street. It is up two flights of stairs in the same building that Larry lives in. Rebecca has a four-room apartment. She is leaving the city with her preteen son Tyrone. We buy most of her furniture. Rebecca leaves us some of her poetry books. There is a complete set of Allen Ginsberg's Pocket Poet poetry books. I had only read a few of his poems. "I don't need them anymore!" Rebecca says. I'm not sure if Ginsberg is really a poet or just a personality of the times. I am overjoyed that she doesn't have a need of her Robert Creeley collection either. Before we move in Tyrone advises me that the block is not too bad if I keep a keen lookout coupled with a readiness to run like hell.

Our front room faces Mary Help of Christians Catholic Church's broad gray steps. They are the hangout for the young men who run a stolen vehicle chop shop. Each car is denuded of all useful parts. It is filled with bagged garbage. Doused with gasoline. Set on fire. The flames rise up a full story. They choke the hot summer night with noxious black fumes. The neighbors line the church steps and party until a lone fire truck lazily backs down the block. Revolving red lights but no siren. Everyone cheers as the firemen pretend to care about hosing the burning hulk. In the morning the blackened skeleton remains festooned with bright shards of garbage melded together. The hulk remains for another week. A city flatbed with a big hook comes by to collect it.

Shelley and I join several Poetry Project writing workshops. Ted and Alice move back to New York City. In 1975 Alice's workshop launches a next generation of poets. Alice's leadership brings us together. Shelley and I make many new friends including Eileen Myles. Bernadette Mayer's experimental writing workshop opens our writing up to present tense.

I read the Allen Ginsberg books. I love his New York School poems in *Planet News* and *Reality Sandwiches*. *Howl* prods me but *Kaddish* really chokes me up. I start to feel a sense of awe for a poet who can be so sexually explicit politically adamant and devotional at the same time. He even lives somewhere nearby. Maybe it is just the right time for Allen to walk into my life.

© McDarrah

I see Allen on the Irv Kupcinet TV show during the 1968 Democratic Convention police riots in Grant Park, Chicago. It is a crude color television and Allen is bright chartreuse. Reading Allen's poetry now humanizes him for me. I read his poems in the Lower East Side and see what he sees and hear what he hears.

Allen needs someone to type for him. He asks Anne Waldman to recommend a typist. She suggests Shelley the secretary at the Poetry Project. Allen stops by East 12th Street to drop the typing off. He mentions that he is looking for a new apartment to rent. We tell Allen about the open apartment one floor up. Our upstairs neighbor Nancy Brugheletta just moved out of a double apartment on the third floor. Shelley does the typing for free because it is to help a political prisoner. Peter Orlovsky and Allen come over the next morning to speak with the landlady Mrs. Seeliger. Allen and Peter charm her. They take apartment number twenty-two/twenty-three at 437 East 12th Street.

Mrs. Seeliger and her quiet husband live directly below Shelley and me. The Seeligers wear grey trench coats everywhere. Mr. Seeliger walks behind her and holds her purse. They cover their windows with newspaper. Winter comes around. Mrs. Seeliger is very careful with heat and hot water. She allows it for one hour in the morning. One hour in the evening. People complain but to no avail. We organize a tenant's organization. Hold the meetings in our apartment so we can stomp on the landlords' ceiling. Allen and Peter come to a few meetings. Allen and Peter's apartment is in the center of the building and has six sunny windows. It is warm all day. Those who live in the dark at the back of the building are nearly frozen solid. Allen and Peter plead for civility and understanding with the Seeligers. We ignore Allen and Peter's peaceful diplomacy. Organize a rent strike. Shelley and I are active in the strike. Pay our rents into an escrow account. All heat and hot water stops after the rent strike begins. After six months of legal battling and no services the housing court judge is rotated out. The new judge orders all escrow funds to be deposited into the court. Shelley and I realize that we will never get

Extract: During my 1950s childhood, I am aware of beatnik jokes. For example:

A beatnik is standing on a corner holding a loaf of bread over his head with one hand. The other hand is stuffed into his pants pocket. A priest passing by says, "Ah Son, I see you have the staff of life in your hand." "Yes," says the beatnik, "and in my other hand I have a loaf of bread."

Maynard G. Krebs
played by
Bob Denver

There is a sitcom on television called "The Life and Loves of Dobie Gillis" with a beatnik character named Maynard G. Krebs. Maynard has a goatee, cutoff sweatshirt, and has an incessant tag line anytime anyone utters the word <u>work</u>. Maynard repeats the word in a high-pitched squeal of disbelief. In early 1960s, my friend Stevie and I dress up as beatniks for Halloween. We have painted goatees, cutoff sweatshirts, berets, and gym shoes without socks. As I descend the stairs of my walkup apartment on East 11th Street to go to work at Allen's, I hear Krebs's screech ringing in my ears – "Work!"

Allen never watches television but after many years of being questioned, he can recall who Maynard G. Krebs is: "Ah yes, the television version of a beatnik from the late 1950s."

East 11th Street has a quirky charm: a view of the Empire State Building; high boxy eastern windows; a shower stall with a skylight; a long footed bathtub in the bedroom; and a sagging tin ceiling. The south-facing view is perfect for Shelley's art studio. It is too good to keep this railroad flat to ourselves, so we grow our family.

Caveman Magazine: composed directly on blue mimeo stencils: slander, misattributions, and scratched-on cartoons.

it all back. So in 1976 we move to a double apartment on East 11th Street. Mrs. Seeliger's Polish epithets follow us down the stairs as a dozen poets carry boxes out the door.

I am back there to work within a year. Come back a professional tenant. I work for Allen. Represent Allen and Peter on the strike committee. I help run these meetings and organize the next legal strategies.

Shelley and I are running Monday Nights at the Poetry Project. Shelley hosts a film series. We publish Frontward Books on the Project's Mimeo machine. Hold collating parties with fellow poet friends. Mail poetry around the country in bundled book rate packets. *Packet Poets*. I write plays with Bob Holman. Everything is always produced by us. Eileen Myles is a challenging poet. Someone to compare oneself to. Eileen and I give a poetry reading where we trade poems back and forth. Eileen has a supple style that employs a casual grace. She tells the listener everything and reveals little. Comrades we all work on creative projects. *The Ear of the Dog* poets' theater at Charas. Early public access poetry cable videos. Scandalous Caveman Magazine. Allen and I help Eileen apply for several grants. Allen really likes Eileen's poetry so I know that he would not favor my poems. I resolve never to show any of them to him.

Persona is to poetry what a hero is to one's life. Heroism is both saving the child from a burning building and facing the drudgery of complex societal demands. The persona in a poem is the living voice that orders the words and arranges the lines. Persona is the interlocutor between the form of the poem and the brain that acquires the poem. The persona to the poet is life as it is led.

Allen creates a cottage industry based on his own persona. Allen is an ancient soul. Wired into consciousness using police agencies antennae. His bardic voice breathes down my neck! I am sort of *a square* brought into an incorrigible beat pad to impose boundaries. I send synoptic letters to Allen. They help me see the bigger picture that derives from the myriad projects.

Oct. 26 '77

Dear Allen,

     I thought I would try to give you a concise state of affairs letter, just to let you know how certain things stand. How about $ matters first. We got a turnoff threat from Con Ed on the single apartment plus a request for $30. deposit. I called them and got them to stay the deposit if I sent the $16. bill in today which I will. The bill on the double apartment is is $30.13 (which includes a $5. fee because someone came to collect and a $10. fee to reconnect) I think that this ($30.13) should be paid promptly to avoid loesing the deposit we put in on Oct. 5. If you want to send that amount in a check to Con Ed I will add the id number and get it paid also. IRS sent an adjusted statement, $121.65 due. I sent Blue Cross its quarterly payment. They (Blue Cross) say that a recent claim for surgery is not covered by your Hopitalization Insurance, if you also have surgical coverage we should let them know. Received both Townhouse deposits and deposited them. A $22.00 refund check from Air New England and was returned by Manufacturers Hanover because the check was not valid after 90 days so cancel ($22. and service charge $1.25) $23.25 from your account. My deposits have totaled $145.50. Phone bill logged in at $164.99. The Master Charge New Balance is $631.88 and minimum payment is $44.00. Cherry Valley School Tax $51.59. The Seeligers have not come around for rent so I sure it can wait until your return. Talked to Anne W. yesterday who expressed abject despair at your not proceeding on the Naropa Lecture for the book of lectures. She says you alone kx have delayed publication. But she sounded despairing in any event. The fall meeting of the Academy of Arts and Letters will be Wed. Nov. 9 at 5:00 PM. There is an RSVP note that offers transport. P.E.N. will sponsor a press conference Nov 3 10 AM at Carnegie Center The subject is repressed writers around the globe and Allard Lowenstein (U.S. Ambassador to the U.N. Human Rights Comm.) will be there. Mel Mendelssohn called and personally hopes you can attend You or I could RSVP to him about it (212) 255-1977. Steve Miller of Red Ozier Press has sent proofs for the chapbook. Miguel Algarin called: wants you to perform at Neuyorican live over WBAI at Midnight on either Nov. 9 or Nov. 23. Brad Halweil (channel 31) wants to interview on Grove book. Peter Chowka wants to update New Age article. High Times wants to do Interview. Grove press sending im many reviews of Journals; all pretty good except one outrageous piece from Tampa Fla. PS. the Kenneth Koch interview in Times is great! So that's enough things. My jury duty is over, I was sequestered one night at the Ramada Inn (must be like Hawaii). Beginning to understand how Lenny Bruce became consummed by the LAW.

Whatever it is, it avails not—distance avails not, and place avails not, …
Crossing Brooklyn Ferry Whitman

Early Cartography: one of my first letters to Allen with many details of the everyday life of Ginsberg. This is followed by another informative letter two years later. The form of the map is crude; it is raw observation and leaves out more than it tells. The spelling is medieval and the sense of time is languorous. A letter can sit in a typewriter carriage for days and not die. But it will curl. Words are places on a map. So too these facsimiles of words are legends to deeper places that reside in the heart.

Hawaii -- that puzzles me. The Ramada Inn on 8th Avenue is the opposite of beautiful. This must be an official "Idiot" exclamation!

Notice that the photo cover fee is a large fee. I lead the paragraph with it because I negotiated the fee and want Allen to see that I pay for myself.

———

"Buddhist Academy" is Allen's term for Naropa. The "puny wages" took place a few years later; "nuts" for one Summer.

———

Manual Ballagas is a student who meets with Allen in Havana in 1965. He does jail time after Allen's deportation. His mother who lives in Florida blames Allen. Allen often tries to help Manual but to no avail.

Dear Allen   July 30 '79

Today is interesting day -- ten years since I Shelley & I first walked into each other's eyeballs.
          Here is mail. with notes on envelopes. there are requests for poems etc. waiting here no rush I trust. Raymond Foye is in NYC and I will speak with him as soon as he returns from South Hampton on Wednesday.   Have an archieve pick scheduled for next week.   I could not find any Sony microphones! I looked in the card board box on your book shelf and in the desk drawers in your bedroom 66 where else? Working now to get caught up an things like tape indexing.
          I deposited into your checking account today $400. from Viking Penguin for Jack's Book photo. Also a credit advice for $13.90 came in for a few English pounds (7/24/79). I will call tomorrow about the 2,000 francs and I think you already know about the $100.00 from Rolling Stone on Jul 16. Also there is $50. from BBC~~which~~ ~~~~ Jul 30. those are all the recent deposits and credits to your checking account. Could you please send a check for the joint account (marked transfer of funds) for $1,000.00 that will cover Sept. rent, Aug & Sept utility, My wages, Lenhart wages, Typewriter repair, tapre recodder repair, and office supplies. Any ?'s please ask but if not please send as soon as possible.! I leave on August 14 and I would like this check to clear before that date.
          Interesting vague offer about Naropa job -- Allen I love your idiosyncrasies (i.e. working for you) however still just getting by $ wise think I would go nuts working in "Buddhist Academy" for xxxx puny wages but since you aren't a sure about what the job would be I don't want to appear negative so keep me informed.
          two days later: rec'd the cop check sent for the fellow in Cuba. Everything I sent his mother came back, certified mail including the return envelope I sent, my cover letter, a COP application form (filled out) and of course the check for $300. There was no note or anything so I assume it is not a good time to do this
          Check no 987. Do you want to do anything now? We (Shelley & I) are very busy mounting several plays including an adaptation of Ted Berrigan's novel, Clear The Range, which Bob Holman & myself wrote. The plays go up Aug 9, 10, 11.

I 'll be in touch soon again about these and other pressing
                              matters

          PS please do send check now

I know that writers often have secretaries: W.H. Auden had Chester Kallman, James Joyce had Samuel Becket. A fledgling writer working for an established writer seems to be a noble occupation. The literary quality of the work enriches the title of secretary. Being the low-paid secretary to a Bardic Poet whose life's work is a cottage industry run out of an apartment by poet cultural workers, I now have a chance to become: the better neighbor, the better tenant, better family man, and the better human being. I learn from one idiotic mistake after another and am given an idiotic amount of time to learn all the rules from Allen Ginsberg.

————

Allen always uses the station name in his return address under the box number (P.O. Box 582, Stuyvesant Station) maybe this is another example of the Theory of Idiots but it is also sweet to remember where we live by remembering the last Dutch governor of New Amsterdam who no doubt would have been happy to hang Allen up by his commie, queer, beatnik, Jewish feet.

Everyday I go to the Post Office. Learn the weekly and monthly bulges to the lines for the pick up window at the Stuyvesant Station. It is a grim drab green scene of despair and poverty. People are demanding their late government checks. They threaten to punch out the hapless clerks. In forty years nothing has changed except for the addition of plexi-bulletproof glass protecting the clerks. I figure it is a punishment post for managers with poor administrative skills.

I cart the mail back to Allen's office. Quickly slice it. Sort it. **Business Literary Personal Junk.** I note down chores to do into a large divided notebook:

Extract: Allen note to Bob.

October 31, 1977: A&S Rec'd books! Write Permissions Letter. Send correct no. of books to Bourgeois. Nov 4. Write Jno. Williams re: Bunting Address -- Naropa 77 / check mail from Columbia Records / CBS Records grey album w/cardboard / Miles English address / Naropa: Books are in the catalog, Space : can you provide accommodation for my students? My class room where? Provision should be made to tape Blake course. Blackboard helpful. Prefer afternoon, Small cassette recorder to play tapes (perhaps can be borrowed) I want to be able to send students to the C.U. Library Special Collections to see reproduction of Blake Prophetic Books in color. Special arrangements -- class in anybody's home -- when am I due Teaching one day at CCNY -- probably midweek. One date on Tuesday March 14 coming up. Have we determined any date? What two weeks? Check with Anne. Call Anne! Tonight!

This detailed note is typical of the care that Allen takes on all assignments. Sometimes I replace manuscripts by troubled poets who have lost their original copies. R'lene Dahlberg sends us Ed Marshall's poetry manuscripts. For years we try to send his poetry back to him. Finally I find a PO Box in Providence Rhode Island. I get a simple postcard reply with a street address on it. I pack the box tightly carry it to the post office. We never hear

———

Iranian Poet outlawed by the Shah. He returned to Iran after the Ayatollah revolution but was arrested and not released until 1982.

———

Harold loves to talk to Allen. He never pays his City Lights bills because he knows that Allen will eventually have to call to nudge him.

———

Peter & Allen *Baby Adoption* Bolding mine. How find baby? Where find baby? Why find baby? I think Allen and Peter are an enlightened gay couple showing a spiritual commitment to each other and jointly living a life dedicated to helping people become sentient. Although I unquestionably accept the deep love that they have for each other, Allen and Peter do not seem like good prospective parents. I am a new father and understand that it is a commitment akin to monogamy. Their poignant request for a baby remains un-acted upon by me; I don't bring it up again.

———

Andreas is Allen's agent to Columbia University deposit. Andreas does the assessment of deposit shipments for free – sort of; in actuality, he keeps all extra copies of all publications that were included in excess of one copy. Strange that there are no first edition books in the deposit when Allen has been so careful to include them! I decide to make the item list myself and organize the boxes. Andreas then provides the assessment from my list.

from him again. We make copies of files such as **Complete CIA** and send them to lawyers. We send the work of Reza Baraheni to PEN Club members and the Washington Post.

Jan. 26, 1978 Extract: Bob's typed up notes on upcoming tasks.

Call Harold Kraucher at Bookazine Book Distributors to collect bill for City Lights Publishers. Tell Barry Gifford (edited As Ever, the correspondence of Allen and Neal Cassady) Kostelanetz received a proof copy. How come I haven't seen it? Don't publish it until I see it! Sent Ed Sanders: many packages of CIA, Leroi Jones letters, re Eldrige Cleaver, Leary Memorandum Jane Fonda Variety Letters, Top Secret FBI. / Write Polish Publishers send proofs find good review list. What is published in Poland since 1965? Copies of books and magazines? How many available in case of visit? Update review list. Create translation list. Add press names from Grove's Journal reviews. **Call Andreas Brown** at Gotham Book Mart. Call PEN Club -- Do you have '73 statement on Abbie Hoffman? Send to Sam Leff. Get Typewriter cleaned. Check out mailbags. Clean desk with AG. "Plutonian Ode" to Aaron Krause, Jan Castro, Jon Cott, Elizabeth Hess & Dave Dellinger, Daniel Barraza. Lists to keep: Books of AG and Magazines, Tapes, Interviews, Essays. Get Ledger. **Peter & Allen** *Baby Adoption*

I usually tick off completed assignments with a check mark. There is no check mark for the "procure baby" assignment. Theory of Idiots?

Send out letters with poems. Essays. Interviews. Fact sheets. Page corrections. Newspaper Articles. Small grants in aid. Contracts. Stage setups. Buddhist axioms. Shedding my idiocy I begin to assert myself in small but redolently paternalistic ways. I remind guests to replace the yogurt they eat. I ask them to take their own sheets and towels to the Laundromat. I start to keep track of the flow of money. A guest takes petty cash for a purchase. Change is now asked for along with a receipt. I also help guests by mailing their boxes of books (post office each time) for them.

Extract: Bob's Assignment List December 1978.

Allen sign First Blues for Mr. Aloisis (to his sister) at Stuyvesant Post Office window 10. Get C.A.P.S and N.E.A. deadlines, Order applications. Organizations forming and formed included: Committee to Stop Spying. Mobilization for Survival, Affinity Ground, CAIFI, Co-Evolution Quarterly, Journal for the Protection of Sentient Beings, Rocky Flats Truth Force, PEN Freedom to Write Committee and WIN. Find German Verlag translator files, arrange interview with London Times, Daily Camera, or for Donald Allen, Screw Magazine, Fernanda Pivano. Retrieve Sulzberger letter re CIA dealing Dope from Columbia.

Some letters are mythic and never found. This one is saved! Then it is copied many times – Theory of Idiots. Allen uses it to eloquently bolster his analysis of CIA Drug trafficking.

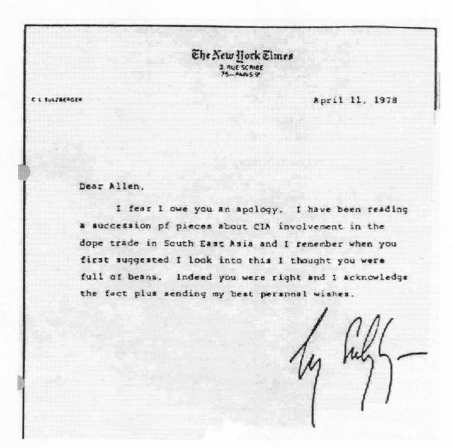

The New York Times
3. RUE SCRIBE
75—PARIS 9

C. L. SULZBERGER   April 11, 1978

Dear Allen,

I fear I owe you an apology. I have been reading a succession of pieces about CIA involvement in the dope trade in South East Asia and I remember when you first suggested I look into this I thought you were full of beans. Indeed you were right and I acknowledge the fact plus sending my best personal wishes.

My increasing savvy and confidence in Allen's circle does not prepare me for the new challenges. Impossible to control Gregory Corso as a guest is one. His rudeness is the most challenging part. He walks into Denise's room in the middle of the night. Gruffly

Equilibrium is both lost and restored in Allen's absences. Allen is the chef; he stirs the soup and throws in new ingredients. He nurtures the scene and leaves as it gets ripe to a bursting point. Allen is so loved and feared that people hold their peace around him and wait for him to leave before falling apart. Allen might be amused by the mischief he both causes and misses. But more likely he is maintaining the only sort of home that he knows.

shakes her out of sleep demanding a cigarette. She screams at him to get out of her room. Denise turns over in bed. He curses her as he sulks back to his bedroom. Not much later she pours a glass of water on the sleeping Gregory. The next day they are not talking. I am unable to establish equilibrium in the apartment. Typically Allen fills the house up with people then leaves to give a poetry reading. All hell breaks loose. More and more I navigate the continual overnight quests daily chores and eccentricities of the boss himself.

3 Generosity All Around

Poem

Attention is a flower – blue impatience
Rested on a star – boyhood
Totally gone between ear buttons
Hurtling through streets of music
Until overheard street cries layered
Random in passion push a simple creation

Raw disquiet echo as pipes hammer
Upstairs leads nowhere to a voice
Singing Buddha full suckled air
Slapping cello string bow & thumb at
Epic electronic heart pick-up socket
Last night is downloaded again
Loves burn deeper while doused

———

The burden of seeing suffering is that one sees it as forms: a hand softly open and pliant, or a distressed phone call, or a five piece sealed envelope. Money carries a murky pool of emotions that recombine jealousy, fear, and pride with mind control. Allen needs to give back to the world, which burdens him so. Because he values money without loving it, money tends to flow to him. In turn, the world is better for it.

ALLEN ALWAYS HAS AN EYE AND A COIN for the Ave. A white haired red-faced drunk beggar or any panhandler. A small check for an old friend. He forms a non-profit grant-giving corporation the Committee On Poetry Inc. Its first task is to raise money to support Lenny Bruce during the district attorneys' harassments in the mid-1960s. Allen uses the money to support dozens of writers. Some receive continual support whereas others only need help occasionally.

The young artist Greg Ruggiero shows up calling for the key to be thrown to him. He needs money to continue drawing on paper plates. Allen is charmed. Writes him a small COP check. Years later Greg edits the important Open Pamphlet series of pertinent uncensored political tractates.

Discretionary grants-in-aid are a formal but private expression for Allen. He keeps the lights on for poets. In bad times bars the landlords from the doors of struggling musicians. Only his closest oldest friends are steady COP recipients. The relief is immediate. No one has to know. Allen's feeling of foiling Moloch by redirecting his own money is a thrilling relief from karmic societal debts.

Allen gives about ten poetry readings a month. This increases throughout his life. Most of the payments earned from readings are donated to Committee On Poetry Inc. Allen also uses the COP money to support his Cherry Valley New York farm. The 81-acre farm is purchased by COP in the late 1960s to provide a communal safe haven. The property is a reclusive meditative space. Being tucked away provides Peter Orlovsky with enough space to be crazy without bothering people. Allen calls it "Peter's Farm" and lets Peter have full control. The countryside provides a gentle sense of seclusion. Loafing is demanded of you until Peter catches you. Writers who visit are expected to clean up their drug/alcohol use. Enjoy the fresh air. Do some farm chores. Eat wholesome food.

Having most of his income diverted into COP keeps Allen's actual earnings low enough to minimize his taxable exposure. He minimizes financial support for America's wars. Allen says that he pays all of his taxes except the "War Tax." This tax is calculated from several categories that add up to the military industrial complex. In addition to shifting income into donations Allen deducts all of his daily expenses. He saves every single receipt. An accordion file of receipts supports his exhaustive personal deductions. Lowers his net income tax even more. War seems to

---

Allen never relaxes on the farm. It is not a place of personal meditation for him. He enjoys being big daddy to his family and being driven to Albany to fly off to a poetry reading and then bringing home the bread. He learns to play pump organs and composes tunes for William Blake's *Songs of Innocence, Songs of Experience.* His only poem about the farm is full of futile problems.

Is letting Peter be as crazy as he likes a good plan? Is he reenacting the pain his mother suffers from doctors? Allen knows his own part in allowing her lobotomy. Peter Crazy? What's the harm?

The only rule at the Committee Farm is: NO NEEDLES!

Allen does not have warm feelings about his government, yet he is a good citizen. The methods of perception he gains from both William and Jack shake the clothes off government. Naked, he shivers. Any warm feeling for government is nostalgically tied to progressive New Deal economic policies, and America's opposition to WWII-era fascism. He is 16 when the world goes naked.

be a constant. Allen hopes to starve war by living on a farm that feeds itself from his poetry.

Harry Smith. Herbert Huncke. Gregory Corso. Each receives regular support from Allen's COP. It is my job to cut the checks. Keep the paperwork. All three men have sharp tempers. Their irascibility is made worse by being near another person of a similar temperament. They do not relish meeting each other at Allen's. Particularly the greater their financial need the greater their impatience. I brashly arrange for them to come over for their checks at the same time. Their stiff attempts to be pleasant to each other quietly amuse me. Each has a dark visage. Herbert is excessively polite to Gregory. Harry shrinks into a chair and gets impatient. Gregory is flamboyant. Sits apart. Waits. He needs help at the bank. I can tell they are all miffed at me. How can they stay mad at me for long? There is always another check to write.

COP keeps a low profile and does not seek publicity. Allen doesn't want unsolicited grant requests. The paperwork is extremely simple. A small grant of under $100 can be sent out without an application as a minor grant-in-aid. We are able to respond quickly. Without any fuss or follow-up reporting. I use COP to umbrella The Committee for International Poetry. My friends and I organize nine international poetry festivals in the 1980s. In the 1990s COP umbrellas new start-up art organizations such as the Charlie Parker Festival and the Howl Festival. Both are public events in Tompkins Square Park.

Paul Violi needs major funds for his newborn son's heart surgery. Allen goes to the emergency fund at the American Academy of Arts and Letters. Allen is careful not to misuse this membership privilege. He can only disburse such a large grant-

Yes I am a check. I write myself out over and over. Through Allen's Bodhisattva training, I attend to the inner Buddhahood in these men. They know me as harmless.

Allen spreads out his mantle, engenders new activities from within his office. New arts groups rooted in Tompkins Square, arise under Allen's umbrella.

in-aid a couple times a year. Later these funds dry up in the early attempts to help with AIDS.

At a restaurant Allen always wants to pay. In fact he needs to pay. It is hard to argue with him. His generosity extends to trust. He trusts old friends extensively. He trusts me although I am young. Many charities and Buddhist sanghas find support in COP.

In large part his income results from his agreeing to do all gigs regardless of fees offered. I am careful not to overwork him. I slowly raise his fees. His trust in me grows. In May 1979 Allen wants me to be able to sign checks myself. We go to the bank to open a joint account. He makes me sit with the bank officer as he paces back and forth behind me. Allen is uncomfortable with actually handling money. Even opening a bank account gives him ants in his pants.

Allen hires poets to do real work. Allen provides them with a needed income. His adoption of the Gandhi Cottage Industry model successfully channels his personal generosity. Ted Berrigan intermittently needs financial help. Allen hires Ted to prepare and edit Peter Orlovsky's book of poetry. Peter's writing is so idiosyncratic that Ted has a hard time discerning which "corrected" version is correct. He soon realizes that it would be best not to correct them at all. Ted ends up searching for the originals of each poem in Peter's journals. Restoring them to their brilliant natural style. He does a masterful job of preparing the manuscript Peter calls *Clean Asshole Poems and Smiling Vegetable Songs.*

Ted is a tall imposing man smiling through missing teeth above a New England seaman's beard. A lit cigarette always rests in the corner of his lips. He wears blue chinos and large pearly

———

Allen has an aptitude for making money; offers just come in. However, Allen doesn't accumulate money; he lives from hand to many mouths.

———

He lives simply and spends money on cabs and meals but otherwise his clothes and furniture are strictly purchased at the Good Will and the Salvation Army.

———

Allen makes me feel dirty sitting in his stead at the banker's desk.

———

The cottage industry model means caring for the workers. In our case the industry is Allen. Poetry is the cottage that contains us. Poets get jobs to help other poets.

———

Without Ted's tremendous effort and care, Peter's true voice might never have been heard.

sweaters covered in cigarette ash. He is accustomed to using pills (uppers and downers) to regulate his body's energies. Ted comes over to work. First he goes to Allen's medicine cabinet. Always finds the pill that makes productive work possible.

Allen mentions to me that the narrow library is overcrowded. I ask if I could engage Ted to cull the books. Allen says "OK." In May 1978 Ted spends several days in Allen's library sedulously looking over all of Allen's books. Ted decides which ones Allen does not need anymore. The fine copies of poetry that need to be kept but are not likely needed for future study are set aside to send to the archives at Butler Library. Many of Allen's books on Hinduism are sequestered to be given away. "Allen doesn't need these anymore," Ted says. I am not so sure so I make a list of the books that are given away. Ravi Singh aka Neil Hackman is a yogi and aspiring poet. Ted suggests that Ravi cart off the Hindu texts. Included among those texts is *The Gospel of Ramakrishna*. Ted opens up a shelf of new space. The piles of books are off the floor. When Allen comes back to town he approves the work. But then he notices that *The Gospel of Ramakrishna* is missing. Allen instructs me to get it back. I call Ravi who graciously returns it.

The *Gospels* are transcriptions of teachings of the Bengali Yogi saint by M a singular devotee. M is Ramakrishna's Boswell. Ramakrishna continuously refers to the dangers of "women and gold" euphemistically referring to women as lust and gold as greed. Allen underlines sections of the book that refer to the Mula (Sanskrit for "root of the spine") but underscores little else. Yet halfway through the book after one more admonition about "women and gold" Allen impatiently scribbles in the margin. "Women and gold are God!" How like Allen to embrace the feared thought and generously extend acceptance.

———
Since Ted has recommended me to my new job, I want to offer him more support.

———
Allen knows that his books are important even if he doubts his own relative importance. He visits every book with his pen. His demeanor calms while cradling a volume in his palms. The library glows like Fort Knox!

———
Nineteen years later, the Ramakrishna book is the only book I take out of his library prior to shipment to the new archives at Stanford University. I take the pale blue volume home. It is a large book with thin pages filled and overfilled with the teaching of the Holy Saint of Bengal. As I slowly read the Ramakrishna discourses, the teachings enlarge my eye for reality and my ability to be both spiritually awake and maintain my duties as a householder, just as Christopher Isherwood's biography of Ramakrishna, *Ramakrishna and His Disciples* (1965) does. Mindfulness can be applied to all desires.

Allen & Women

When I first work for Allen Ginsberg I notice that there are many hetero-romantic love letters by women. One woman writes twice a month. These are forceful letters that promise to transform Allen. Overcome "this problem of homosexuality." These letters are perfumed and often from Europe.

I published one of these letters in parody magazine Caveman.

Allen does not hate women but. . . Allen has a terrible habit of not paying attention to women. Not remembering their names. Not introducing them to his famous friends. Forgetting to add their names to photograph captions. I try to fill in the gaps when I can. I introduce women to him. Note their names for captions. I try to make excuses for Allen. I naively call him a benign misogynist. I have also met many women who will never forgive Allen for his brusque treatment towards them.

I use "benign misogynist" to poet Barbara Barg and am quickly chastened, "Well, that sounds like an oxymoron, doesn't it?"

There is a sizable Whitmanic all-encompassing come hither and dally side to Allen's nature. He is calm and open to almost everybody. Women and men alike encounter Allen and remember it. Misogyny is not a word of degrees. There is no way to account for how Allen can be a misogynist and not dismiss all women intellectually. Yet Allen does value the intelligence of the women who work for him.

For years, Allen calls my wife "Shirley."

Allen has had girlfriends. He always remembers to complain that Rambling Jack Elliott steals his girl but the girl's name alas is gone. Does he remember the girl who thinks he is a little coo-coo in 1953? He complains that Alene damages his cock. His descriptions of female genitalia in his poetry are alienating. Women are the rivals for the young men he pines for. Women are fierce adversaries. He and Andrea Dworkin just scream at each other. In the film *Fried Shoes & Cooked Diamonds* Allen narrates in mock seriousness that if he were straight he would like to marry Anne Waldman. She gracefully dives into the swimming pool at Varsity Townhouses Naropa.

Read his poem *This Form of Life Needs Sex*.

Allen's poetry continues to liberate teenagers and adults of all sexes.

Allen is unsure why there are so few female writers in the Beat Generation. One reason is that society does not allow women to embrace a dangerous path like poetry. Poetry can force a free-spirited daughter into the nuthouse. Perhaps Allen himself is an amalgam of female stereotypes. He has a nurturing concern for people's well being. Allen feeds soup to his household and students. He is faithful to friends. His love is as much spiritual as it is male. When young he tries to love women but he ends up fooling himself. He dotes on young men. He is delighted when anthologies of women Beat writers are issued. But he is not off the hook. Late in his life the inclusion of women has become expected. He allows his staff to add women to mini anthologies. Collections of photographs. A poetry reading series. He works closely with women in his own home. I hire women to be assistants. He treats them with respect. **Allen appreciates their work and increases their responsibilities.** He listens to their advice.

When female students at the Kerouac School confide to Lorna Smedman that it makes no sense to study with Ginsberg, she replies. "No you must take him and get the good stuff and pay no mind to what you can't use." There is still enough good stuff in Allen to merit an approach to his words.

Allen is not a hater of women. The few women who are his friends enjoy the same attention that his male friends do. There are just many more male friends. He champions Eileen Myles' poetry because he likes it as poetry. Whitman includes women in his major poems to achieve a pan-sexuality. Allen doesn't do this. Is this a sign of a competing form of liberation? Allen is unapologetically gay. Allen transforms gender into

Gay love and straight love have merged into real love and not a set of competing jocular jingoisms.

The oppression of women stems from all forms of men: straight and Allen's nearsighted gayness!

_____

Some of my friends thought I might be a Boswell to Allen's Johnson. "Keep a daily diary!" they chide. But that is not the level of my devotion. Nor do I know what my devotion consists of. I work hard to distinguish myself from the Bard. I share less and less of my life with him. I cling to the mantle of secretary and go home to a separate life. Even if I am stunting my personal growth as a poet, poetry is still my devotion and I write my poems on domesticated delicacies and write polemics on the nature of men's desires and women's desires. Being a writer on my own terms is acceptable to Allen; he still never gets to read my writings.

_____

I teach the college student callers how to use Student Activity funds or grant write to get a new short reading series partially funded. I advise how to frame the budget and how to write the appeal emphasizing the current funding trends. Of course, Allen gets the reading and I get 10%.

self. He does use a feminine form of intelligence in his poetry. His sexual expression is structured to engender a feeling of liberation. Allen finds the key in the window. He gives permission to change one's consciousness. The threatening mind-traps to be burned in the 21st Century are: Misogyny. Homophobia. Race Privilege. Patriarchy. Aggression. Society continues to broaden the distinctions regarding both gender identity and sexual preference. I think Allen would be charmed by and would learn from the discussion. Great women poets are a possibility for Allen. He offers to marry Alice Notley soon after Ted dies. It seems he feels a responsibility. Alice is speechless. Women are a possible outcome of his spiritually charged sexual openness. Allen gives a key to all who hear. Allen conceals his modesty but not his sexuality. He is a Gay pioneer because of his candor. He lifts the weight of the world onto himself as he enters it. *The weight of the world is love.*

_____

Sure it hurts. I am distancing myself from an experience I fear. I recall my mother distancing herself from me. I am five and my nine-year-old brother falls deathly ill, and later again a distance is forced by my father who worries I might become gay. I learn distance at home.

Allen's entire office is built around the concept of generosity. Most of my clerical work is related to Allen's social activism. I am expected to help those who call. Allen's office is an arts-servicing organization. Someone calls up and asks how to start a poetry reading series in their hometown or at their school. I explain how to apply for matching grants. Share current funding buzzwords. I explain the loans at the Author's Guild. The emergency funds at the PEN club. I note which debts are most convincing to funders. I help writer friends of Allen's find emergency funds. We have COP. Allen contributes directly into the fund. Other donors pass the money through the tax-free conduit. Sometimes we pay a writer's bills directly if they cannot be trusted to hold the money without redirecting its use. Helping junkies to pay conventional bills is a task requiring nerves of steel and plenty of brains.

People often call for help in finding a literary agent or publisher. Here Allen cannot be as generous as he would like to be as he is afraid of receiving manuscripts. He isn't sure himself how the publishing industry works.

Allen's fast delegating of responsibility to me is generous. Does he know something about me that I don't? I am not long in his employ before he writes to Ken Lohf director of Butler Library Special Collections Columbia University to give me personal authority over the entire collection. I have the privilege of granting permission to others to make use of the collection. I visit Mr. Lohf. Hand him Allen's hand-written letter. His eyebrows shoot up. He looks at me a long moment. Leaps up to show me the stacks. Utility shelves hold the Special Collection of rare books and precious manuscripts. Allen's collection is neatly boxed in rows. Parts of the collection have been cataloged by Columbia. Subsequently purchased. Ken Lohf asks me if Gregory Corso is currently writing. "He is washed up. Isn't he?" I am shocked. I assure him that Corso is creating new poetry. Allen's deposit is the most actively used collection at Columbia. Researchers and scholars either call or write to Allen. I handle the arrangements.

Allen generously creates jobs that pay wages. The work is exacting. One task that everyone including myself toils over is cataloguing Allen's recordings. Barry Miles creates a complex Ginsbergian system to index all recordings. The first two numbers indicate the year of composition. Next a single capital letter indicates the type of tape it is. Poetry reading. Workshop discussion. Interview. Master tapes from recording sessions. Telephone conversations. This letter is followed by the number of tapes in the series. A slash is inserted. Followed by a three-digit index number per year. Concluding with an identification letter

_____

Allen is a man of faith in that he has faith in other people. I don't realize that Allen has faith in me until that moment in Ken Lohf's office. Ken's pointed question about Gregory of course is obviated by Gregory's lack of career anyway. *All washed up*? What an ugly phrase! And Gregory has much more myth and poetry in him. Gregory has to short sell himself. The financial demands on him are habitual. After selling a holograph manuscript of a published book more than twice, that source of revenue is closed off.

_____

So 73A2/001C tells me that this tape is a poetry reading (A) recorded in 1973 and there are two tapes in this series – furthermore, this is tape number one for the year and the tape's format is cassette (C).

to indicate the format of tape. Reel to reel or cassette.

New tapes arrive in the post office box every week. The manually assembled lists of tapes are sorted by years. It proves awkward and inefficient but Allen treasures the system. It mimics his idiosyncrasy to recall information in holistically manageable clumps. The young poet must compose the label. Paste the label. Write the label content directly onto the box. Write it onto the actual plastic housing of the tape. Type up the listing. Replace the list in a large three-ring notebook. Allen's performance agreement stipulates Allen receive a taped copy of every poetry reading or class discussion. We rarely listen to any of the tapes.

Allen does improvise on stage. He notes it in his calendar. We then note it on the tape when it arrives. He is never certain when he might give the best reading of any single poem. It is safest to have copies of all readings. Allen hopes for a "best of" collection of his poetry readings. Unfortunately we do not require that the reading be recorded on high quality equipment. Readings are usually recorded by rudimentary cassette machines with built in condenser microphones. Allen also insists on receiving copies of every interview tape. If someone is good at keeping the tape catalog they go on to picking up the mail. Typing up the journals. In my first year I do all the office tasks from typing up new poems to tossing out hideous smelling foods from the fridge. The phone rings a lot. I take control of the calls.

Allen's generosity extends to my pay rate. It is modestly adequate for survival. Allen knows when it is time for me to earn more. He looks up at me and says "Couldn't you use a little more now?" I gratefully reply that I have been holding off asking him. He is aware of my growing family. Allen is proud that he can

_____

True to the 20th century's gift of recording and the advent of the post nuclear age, Allen learns to invest in himself and assume the best versions of each poem can be captured and mixed to create a *cream* edition. He has a digital concept in an analogic world. Recording is a part of recovering the original thought. The tape is the backbone of the interview because few can possibly take accurate notes. He demands the tapes to check them himself!

support us. He cares about our viability. It is easy to take Allen for granted. He is so generous.

I hate those who steal from Allen. I refuse to think that anyone would. To steal from one who works so hard to give it away displays man's lowest behavior. I am less forgiving than Allen. I continue to dislike these thieves. Allen shrugs his shoulders as if to remind me that the slight is small. The injury to myself for carrying the hurt so many years is more serious. Allen can always find an excuse for those who steal. Addiction. Deprivation. Hunger. Abandonment. He has known these conditions. He keeps them close in his life in an effort to never experience them again.

Munificence includes the benevolent eye. It includes the eye that does not feel jealous of another's fortune. How safe I sleep with my wife and baby with Allen Ginsberg one block away. Allen turns towards me while seated at the brown plywood desk. He is penning a severance letter to Richard Elovich. Allen wants to continue to work with me. He tells me that Richard is more from Burroughs' circle. I am more a poet. Friendlier.

Allen seems especially giving to Peter Orlovsky. City Lights publishes Peter's poetry book. I organize the publication party at the Gotham Book Mart. Peter supplies gallons of apple cider from wild apples, which he hand-picked and pressed on the farm in Cherry Valley. It is a happy and sober moment that is not to last. But generosity is all smiles in the winter of 1978.

Richard is the Ginsberg secretary I am filling in for.

The Gotham Book Mart
and
City Lights Books

cordially invite you to a reception in honor of

PETER ORLOVSKY

to celebrate the publication of his book

CLEAN ASSHOLE POEMS & SMILING VEGETABLE SONGS
Poems 1957 - 1977

Monday, December 18th, 1978, 5 to 7 pm
GOTHAM BOOK MART GALLERY
41 West 47th Street, New York

Clean Asshole Poems & Smiling Vegetable Songs by Peter Orlovsky, (City Lights Books, 261 Columbus Ave., San Francisco, CA 94133. $3.95 paper)

WE ALL ARE PETER ORLOVSKY

putting paper through the type writer as I please
after reading twenty year volume of verse & song
composed and sung from toe nail tongue
didactic like a subway roar
cheerful as an asshole of snow
heart torn self inquiry tracing lima beans to my heart
Oh the bad Peter Orlovsky!
his book is out and he is such a grouch!
Denise wants him to buzz off the planet
(not a nice thing to say to Denise he just critizes!)
Allen thinks Peter is on speed
            again disconnected
Peter's mother wants to sue Peter and Ferlinghetti
            defaming her character!
Oh beautiful book such bad news for Ocean of Generosity
raspberries muttering evil thoughts this cold Cherry Valley day
            Peter warm in New York!
writing more poems than the Pope!
this Peter Or lov sky doing leg lifts in a cold bathtub
            ready to clean inbetween my beans!
            ALL DAY
night seeking straight answers in venetian blinds
hugging Julius who still likes him!
Peter Peter we love you! Monster of print!
demanding receiver & telegraph of apple juice!
for those who only study the words
secrets spoke from the mummy in the heart
bring them wisdom of infestation
            a travel book to Paris, Cairo
Bombey and Jerusalem
a rattling body frame in Cannes
early lovers earlier vould be lovers (Your Mother!)
old man lovers young Jesus pisser
if genius is a little person who stands by your door
genius stands by each page more bold than numbers!
let's call up Jenine!
oh young Peter concentrated on a bird grip
to Peter grizzled in the garden caked in song butter
We kneel to be inbetween the covers of this Clean Asshole
loving wriggle steady head perfect pitch teacher no soul!

                              December 27,1978

                              -- Bob Rosenthal

William Burroughs as a parallel universe just an easy walk down Bowery. James Grauerholtz is William's secretary. Although we have the same title our jobs are very different. James runs direct interference for William. Protects him from an increasingly inquisitive world. My job is more like an aid-de-camp. I prioritize new business but never shelter Allen. I rely on him to make his own decisions. Allen sees his life as a business. I realize it is best for me to keep our relationship business-like. How?

1.   I am not likely to jump into bed with him.
2.   Allen has his own favorite young poets. I have to help them whether I like their poetry or not. It would be harder if I were jealous.
3.   I am unconcerned with Buddhism so I stay out of Allen's membership with his sangha.

This way I can ease in and out of Allen Ginsberg's world. I can be called at all hours. Yet never end up having to go to Allen's apartment in the middle of the night.

I learn that I have to do whatever Allen says. This helps me succeed but also results in early disappointment. It is my idea to apply to New York State artist grants for both Allen and Peter. I do the work. They both win! I also apply to the NEA Artist Fellowship. They are set at $10,000 each. Allen offers me 10% of any awards actually granted. Both Allen and Peter receive fellowships too. This is fortunate for me since Shelley and I are living just above the poverty line. I need a boost in revenue. Allen graciously gives me my agreed percent of his award but he begs me not to take any of Peter's. "Oh see. Peter has never had any money of his own. And having this award will do a lot to keep his mental state well grounded." Without hesitation I defer "Of course of course!" Within a few months Peter gifts his lump sum to Chöygam Trungpa Rinpoche. At first it angers me. Why do I believe Allen? Soon I realize that I need to apply the benevolent eye. Bask in my own contentedness at having been smart enough to fill out their applications. The lesson of generosity is that

----

Allen leaves me notes from his late night work at the desk. The broad window at the end of the desk emits honking Spanish chatter. Sodium vapor streetlights cast ghostly reflections that frame the open window with Hawthornian moonlight. Allen is in his tighty-whities and sleeveless undershirt hunched over the glow of his father's desk lamp, which is a fluorescent circle around a large magnifier. Allen pores over a letter, fountain pen in hand, and makes action notes. Most often his notes are clear and complete and at times they teach me some nuances of courtesy that need to be adhered to in a subtler manner.

power-sharing changes reality.

In the years before word-processing one has to be an excellent typist to produce a clean typed page. We at Ginsberg Cottage Industry are anything but perfect typists. We liberally apply the pen. Pray for legibility. As we write slowly the lines grow bolder with flowing ink. Corrections and inserts seem to jump out at the reader. The office evolves from hand-written copy to manual typewriter to electric typewriter to electronic typewriter to a word processor typewriter to the first Macintosh 512 with tractor feed ImageWriter.

As the office grows in technological sophistication Allen grows in sophistication in the use of the pen. He cherishes his Montblanc pens (especially the later models that use ink cartridges). All of Allen's shirts have blotchy pen leaks beneath the breast pocket. Allen is a true man of letters. He goes to bed with his journals every night. Strokes the pages with pens leaving his desires and kenotic lines for poems. His pens grow more expensive. He never outgrows his preference for the marbled wide ruled composition blank books. He fills and dates them by the scores.

Allen hand-writes all of his works. His sense of capital lettering is utterly emphatic. Devoid of any consistency. Allen uses fountain ink to expressively write his words. His use or misuse of commas just has to be followed. If I do insert an appropriate comma Allen is sure to circle it and strike it out. I learn to trust the force.

There are some words that pleasure Allen to misspell. He insists on arcane spellings. Tanger (Tangier). *Thompkins* (Tompkins) Square. *Pyjamas* (pajamas). *Travellers* (travelers).

————

I feel that aiding Allen makes a more powerful person out of me.

————

In fact, Allen is downright "scrivacious"! He writes in almost all of his books; he leaves me written messages rather than oral instructions.

This report to Allen summarizes my first two years' efforts on his behalf:

Random House | 800
High Times | 200
Viking | 400
Esquire | 525
—————
1,625

October 9 1979

Dear Allen,

    Here is a summary report of roughly my last year working for you.

    first of all my common duties have included collecting the mail, reading the mail and sorting it and answering as much as I could on my own. I have also conducted your correspondance as per your instructi--ons . Other routine matters have become taking care of the 12 th st. accounts, paying rent, utilities, collecting rent from Cliff Fyman and overseeing the well being of both apartments (i.e. rewiring kitchen in #24, repairing door on #23), I have also taken my own initiatives in regards To organizing your files, I have moved the files, created new ones, and straightened them out at times. Others routine works includes being there to answer the phone and to make phonecalls. I keep track of things borrowed and things broken and things stolen. Well you have a good idea of the routine in any case.

    This last year I worked hard organizing the Peter Orlovsky Book party which included money negotiations w/ Gotham, City Lights, and yourself. I have made two shipments to the Columbia deposit, one of thirty boxes and one of six or seven, both shipments were completely catalogued for future office work use. I manage, at times, the COP account and completely handled the confusing and messy Jakov Lind business. I prepared Ray Bremser's manuscript for Cherry Valley ed. As you know

My summary encapsulates a comprehensive service that I am yet not aware is my lot to give. My advice at the end is correct and is even truer in his last years.

we both worked very hard to organize the Spring Europe trip but by the end it was mostly in my hands. I would say that was almost three months solid work, or at least on my mind, with things to do. Certainly I took much of the worring upon myself. That work included negotiating fees, travel tickets and dates. It included confirming all arrangments and finalizing them into a book form with complete instructions on what to follow up on once in Europe — OK enough on that — you recall it. I have worked with several people doing research at Columbia and I negotiate on several occasions fees for use of photographs. (High Times, Esquire, Viking) I have taken the responcibility or hiring and supervising people to work for us. I have had to resist other people's abuses of our mutual account and resisted any of my own temptations although Allen I know I don't have to steal from you because I can honestly request aid. I managed the Cop tax matters and helped Wilen some with your taxes. I have written CAPS and NEA grants for both You and Peter and xxxxxxx & edited your poems for these applications. I have done emergency work for Naropa and Shambala. (book ordering, nagging authors) I have worked with on the Amer. Academy of Arts and Letters and done two large mailings in this regard, the latter mailing composed jointly by you and I. I also represent Peter O. (resume, readings, tours)

    Allen I have worked two years for you now and I want to say I both enjoy and learn from it. The job has not become stale to me and niether have you. I sometimes give free advice and this is it: Relax about the neurotic/karmic system about this office, we can work slowly to turn each thing about as long as we (esp. you)

        stay healthy and creative.

Thanks Allen
love Bob Rosenthal

Acquaintence (acquaintance). *Developement* (development). *Aggrivating* (aggravating). *Asside* (aside). *Neucleus* (nucleus). *Volkswagon* (Volkswagen). *Dispite* (despite). The common poetic misspelling of *thru* or *tho*. Allen also consistently misplaces the apostrophe in contractions such as *does'nt* or *have'nt*. His eye for form overlooks deeds of misspellings. I am ill equipped to check him. Therefore we hire more poets to help. Ones that can spell.

Poets are fiery creators and often abide on the edges of style. My inability to spell stems from dysgraphia, which means the brain does not "see" a word in the mind (lacks a screen). The poor speller relies on memory and pronunciation to form a spelled word. This can be an aid to poets by eliminating a screen between the poet and the page. The words just appear while being beaten out of a rhythm in the brain.

The biography draft for 1977 below illustrates how Allen corrects for accuracy, economy of style, and personal expression:

Bob retype corrected Xerox Copies to City Lights & Rothschild as "Addenda" to Biographical Précis.

Being square to the hip world means keeping people honest. This is a hard gig for me as sometimes those people are my teachers (Ted Berrigan) or a Beat literary legend (Gregory Corso) or a boyfriend of Allen's or a visitor from Europe who needs a bed and then brings home a lover who makes long phone calls to Poland. But that is just a layer in the karmic neuroses that makes life continuously amazing even in its dull routine.

I feel like a minor wise guy walking one block to work. Scooting around to the post office to wait in line for Box 582. At Allen's I meet visitors freeloaders young men of the night who wake up at 1pm. I am good at paying for myself. I earn four to five thousand dollars in a year. I bring in over twenty thousand dollars by applying for grants. Charging for readings. Setting fees for photograph use in publications.

The 1970s are a special time in New York City. Shelley and I arrive exactly as the Lindsay Years conclude. The city is in economic free-fall. President Ford famously refuses to help the economically strapped city. The entire country seems to relish the plight of New York City. It is dismissed as ethnic. The city is much more. Crime. Poverty. Crack cocaine. Wannabe artists. Drug users. The ethnic populations are working hard to stay alive. Allen can afford his small home office. Bob Dylan has a small office downtown that collects his mail at Peter Cooper station. William Burroughs has an office/loft on the Bowery. Painters have offices. Small non-profit peace organizations have offices. In twenty minutes I can walk from Burroughs' bunker to Robert Franks' loft (Great Jones) or Peter Cooper Station (4th Avenue) to the PEN Club (Spring Street). The city is peppered with survival work opportunities that don't pay much. Working at the Strand Bookstore. Reading books on tapes for the blind. Proofreading. The city offers only enough to live in it.

Naomi Saltzman is our contact at the Dylan office. She is a genuine New Yorker friendly and unreserved. Allen respects Dylan's privacy. Always waits for Dylan to contact him. Allen's acquaintances often want Allen to forward messages or requests directly to Dylan. Allen always refuses. We restrict our contacts with Dylan to calling Naomi. Naomi always gets back to us when we have a real question or a request to "Dylan World." It is exciting to think of all the kindred arts workers walking the streets. Not driving. Home to the post office to the copy shop back to post office. The telephones are big and black and have rotary dials that click rapidly as we reach out to each other in deliberate camaraderie.

Peter's brother Julius is living with the boys. He looks like Peter but is smaller. He has deep jowls. A slack jaw hangs below soft large sad eyes. His medium length hair seems to stick straight up. Bends a bit at the tips. He wears gray chinos that hang loosely on his slender frame and wears a belt even looser. He never means to intrude yet he always does. I work at the big desk in the front room. I listen to music on the radio. He comes in and says "Bob would you like me to turn that off?"

"No Julius. I am listening to it. If you do not care for it you may turn it off."

"Did I say that I did not care for it?"

"No! Well then leave it as it is."

Julius walks back in fifteen minutes later and begins asking again "Would you like me to turn this off?"

I laugh hard. "Yes Julius I would like you to turn it off."

He gives me a toothy grin of tobacco-stained teeth flecked with tobacco bits. Julius never cusses. Denise and Anne try to outwit Julius. The girls interrogate him to trick him into saying a swear word. He plays happily along. They are good. I would have been on all fours swearing like a dog but Julius maintains his poise. He never utters the sought-after naughty word. He stands in the big window on a rainy afternoon. Watches the pigeons line

Julius appears to be catatonic but in actuality, he is sagacious in a very quiet way.

up under the eaves of Mary Help of Christians Church across the street. He stares. Distractedly smokes cigarettes. All of a sudden the reverie is broken. "Bob what do you think those pigeons are thinking?"

"Julius. I don't know. What do you think they are thinking?"

He smiles but does not turn his head to tell me.

The apartment is an internationally mapped vortex of visitors who keep popping up like headlines on the Time*s*. Allen is a homebody. Also he is a persistently arriving and departing visitor. I run down the steps to help him carry up his heavy bulging Danish schoolbook bag and black harmonium case. After a very long absence he plops down at our desk. Sees the piles of his mail ready to read. It is neatly prioritized and stacked out of the envelopes. He leans back. Grasps the stringy hairs along the sides of his head. Starts pulling hard while loudly exclaiming "Ah Karma! Ah Karma!"

————

When Allen drops out the skies from airlines, he calls from the airport. I keep an eye out onto 12th Street to await his cab.

Tues Feb 12 '80 Bob -- Enclosed W2 form from 1979 Naropa Did PEN retype my letter? Send copy of original appeal to Pen to Grinspoon whom I saw in Cambridge. Check if RIPS can send me list of illustrations here. Teaching Campion & Quantative meters. Settling back in Boulder with another horrific pile of mail -- Allen W.I.N. sent copies here thanks Did Ed Sanders get a copy of the PEN Club Report in Xerox??

4 Argument: How to Free the Prisoner

from *Looking Up*

things were looking up from the pillow
gray slabs of dream matter floated over my eyes
plain pine boards aged with grayed sufferings
materialized into walls and roofs and bunks
floor to ceiling death smelling sweat
I was walking back and forth between dream
the reality of this dream and the morning . . .
    the joy of life must exist
    here at everywhere coordinated
    with stripes of
    terror but to still be alive
    that is truly a dream

————

When Shelley and I are young and newly clothed in love, we do not fight. We strive only to please each other. The first argument is the invention of anger. I comment that I think that Sophia Loren is beautiful. "Oh, would you sleep with her if you could?" So the truthful answer is yes. But the smart answer is no. In fact, the answer is of no importance. The argument never ceases.

Isn't the emotional growth in life borne out of struggle? The Judaic culture embraces the tenets of argument and so does Western critical thinking. Allen uses his razor-like poetic acumen to focus on a single tenet: how the world could be a better place. By the way, the answer is always yes.

MAN IN SOCIETY OFTEN NEEDS CORRECTION. This is the crux of religion and literature. The human as character is one that extends. Then embodies. Makes an error. Learns from the mistake. Or doesn't. Changes the behavior. But nothing is simple. People languish in the primary phases of error. They manifest it in argument. Allen bravely speaks out about his political views and sexual choices. He is extremely outspoken in the casual language of everyday bickering.

There is a pillar of righteousness in Allen that needs strident expression. He often raises his voice to startle a novice. "You didn't bring batteries!" Makes an "outrageous" suggestion to force social awareness. "Because I am a fairy, Madam!" Calls out playground crudities. My experiences as a new father help me label minor verbal explosions as just that. Small children will fall over in paroxysms of laughter at any mention of poop. Allen is rooted in this primal stage of pre-self-correction.

Paranoid visions of FBI surveillance rule Allen's mother. Not paranoid Allen joins with others to retrieve all the government secret documents on the anti-war movement and its leaders. Under the *Freedom of Information Act* individuals can request papers. They arrive with sections redacted in bold black marker. When many people request the same document the censor varies. The censored parts of the original slowly start to emerge through comparison. Eventually the complete documents are assembled organized shared. Allen has two filing cabinets stuffed with photocopies of the most important individual papers. The most persuasive are filed into a **Cream FBI** file. Allen saves everything so friends send papers to him to be saved.

Allen treasures the products of his passion and the products of American culture. The buttery photocopies transport Allen. Some are horrified "Allen! You did what?" He opens his hand. Marvels at his viscous grey fluid. Not wiping it away. He proudly shows it off. In *On Neal's Ashes* he ponders the weight of the semen cream in his palm. Sees his lover's skeleton. The Cream FBI files are the most impregnating documents of the congregated lot.

The juvenile sexual and intellectual energy in Allen exercises itself in argument. Often his arguing takes the form of personal grudge matches with columnists. Politicians. He raises his voice. His finger points to the sky. Allen's face emits a deep red glow. He learns that being loud and "in one's face" is not the most effective way to be convincing.

Here is a glimpse into Allen's prophetic nature. When arguing, he goes deep within, his eyes roll inward. He ascends Mount Sinai and receives words. Thus he is always correct without always being right. The glow settles about him when the disagreement has passed; good to last until he needs to refill his chalice.

The central tactic to making an argument is to never be inaccurate. Be aware. One exaggeration. One unsupported assumption. One erroneous statistic. Invalidates an entire argument. The most insidious tendency in argument is to exaggerate. "You always do such and such." "Thousands of writers have been arrested!" Maybe only 108 are arrested. Facts must be demonstrable. Allen is very meticulous about the ordering of the facts in an appeal. He creates drama with arguments and climactic consequences. He follows with an addendum of supporting documentation.

Often an issue only requires a letter. I compose those letters. Send them to Allen to approve. I include a few Buddhist catchwords in my appeals. *Grounded* and *Mindful* are easy to slip into arguments as they make common sense. Allen tinkers with my sentences a little. I retype it and put my code "BRComp" on the lower left corner. Allen signs it. Scholars will not confuse its real authorship. It gives me pleasure to compose a signed letter to the Governor of New York knowing it will be answered. Allen is a citizen of record. One who should be answered personally. I help him send many more letters out than he could on his own. I share in Allen's power. This is not an element of control but rather a more powerful fire whose light exposes societal injustice. Fighting anonymously truly brings truth to power.

A few personal causes stretch out over years. One such case is David Solomon who is convicted for intent to distribute LSD in England. He is an author on drugs and drug culture. He is inaccurately labeled a drug distributor. David has been in prison for about a decade. Allen is trying to improve his prison conditions

Allen enforces an office rule that all factual statements in a position essay have to be either eye-witnessed or corroborated by two differing sources before use.

Issues: clean up nuclear waste dumps; release Timothy Leary from jail; increase book acquisition in Newark libraries; end the death squads in Central America; decriminalize drug addiction; abolish the draconian practice of capital punishment.

It would be more accurate to label David a psychedelic propagandist. He is caught holding a large amount of the raw ingredients for LSD. This breaks the argument into a few pieces. He is dangerous for his writings as they might influence people to use psychedelics. He has not distributed much LSD and might be guilty of intending to distribute. The issue then is that this is a political crime, as LSD is outlawed as spiritually insidious. The final issues are the length and conditions of David's incarceration.

Allen synthesizes these issues into a single compelling demand for release now. I learn that these cases are the bedrock of our freedom as government intransigence perpetually erodes real liberty.

David moves to New York City and we help him get his apartment by posting a rent guarantee. Having been a back scene builder of David's appeal, I am thrilled to really meet him. We feel a bond that only stems from being involved in a cause that has real merit.

by lobbying for an immediate release. The case exposes the harsh "Official Secrets Act in England" that prevents the prisoners from owning a pen or paper. Allen helps David by writing letters to the British officials involved with the Solomon case. Allen and Peter arrange to visit David in the maximum-security prison. Allen compiles a report. Allen's narrative delineates a typical day in David's life in hour-by-hour increments. I type up the narrative. Assemble some of Allen's photographs. The next section is a straightforward accounting of the original legal case. The final argument is a stern statement of concern for David's health under severe penal treatment. Easier incarceration or an immediate release is the clear goal of the appeal. It concludes with an addendum of photocopies of relevant legal documents and press accounts of Solomon's trial. Allen writes a new cover letter. We end up with a packet that's about ten pages long. I have to get that all proofed. Verify every statistic. Head to the copy shop to make multiple sets of the appeal. Cart it to Post Office. Mail them. The prison officials in England. The media that covered the case previously. Friends and lawyers who keep up-to-date with each other's causes. The campaign does not bring about an immediate response. The insistence of Allen and others keeps David safe and healthy in prison. No doubt the campaign facilitates his eventual release a few years later. I am reminded that real power is ruled by the unseen. Unheralded people can make the world react to a truer kind of leadership.

The case of Charles Culhane and Gary McGivern creates long letters. Benefit performances. A surprising alliance of Allen and William Buckley Jr. Charles (Chuck) and Gary are being transported in the New York State justice system. They are headed to a court appearance regarding a gas station robbery. An additional prisoner overpowers a guard and causes the vehicle to crash. In the confusion Chuck and Gary escape. They are soon rearrested. They learn that the officer died. So did the third prisoner. They are charged with murdering a police officer. Now they are convicted and sentenced to die in the electric chair. Chuck is a poet. Allen becomes aware of his poems from prison and investigates the case. Gary marries Marjorie Culp. Marjorie champions their cause for a reduction in the death sentence to life with possible parole. Allen writes letters to the Governor and collaborates with William Buckley on an appeal. William and Allen enjoy defying everyone's expectations by joining together on a cause. The frequent appeals keep the prisoners safe and ultimately alter the sentence. Hasten their release.

Allen and his office staff are invited to *The National Review* Christmas party. Allen Peter and I go to the narrow ground floor apartment that is their office. Scotch is abundant and I have a few. I remember circling Allen as he has a fierce argument with a young man. They both are adamantly gesticulating. Hurtling arguments at each other. Dinesh D'Sousa is a Dartmouth student activist on the infamous conservative *Dartmouth Review*. He directly links to *The National Review*. D'Sousa gives Allen much virtuous heated pleasure. In two short years D'Sousa plays an important role in the Reagan presidency. He authors a scurrilous attack on the National Endowment on the Arts entitled *The NEA of Pornography*. He attacks the NEA fellowships to some writers particularly the poets. Most particularly Peter Orlovsky. Just the title of Peter's book *Clean Asshole Poems* makes D'Sousa's case. The NEA takes a strong drubbing in Congress based

———

Allen creates his non- profit to raise money for the Lenny Bruce defense fund. Bruce is being arrested for obscenity on the stage by District Attorneys in multiple states. Bruce pursues his legal battles until near broken; he fixes himself too big a shot. Allen follows the law and always strives to change society by amending laws. Yes, Allen is arrested for civil disobedience; isn't that proof of a huge respect for due process?

———

Chuck now works in a non-profit organization that lobbies to abolish the death penalty.

———

In the cab home, I am drunkenly vociferating against Dinesh. Allen is charmed, "Usually you are so quiet. I like you this way!"

on this article. The fellowship panelists are never given so much freedom again.

Allen is an active member of the PEN Club. Serves on their executive board. He works closely with the *Freedom to Write Committee*. I work on appeals for writers in prison in Turkey. The Soviet Union. Iran. I take the basic information from the committee. Rework it with Buddhist clarity that reflects Allen's temperament. The letters open with a little rebuke but appease later to fully engage. Allen meets with writers on his overseas poetry tours. Reports back to *Freedom to Write*. He is dutiful in making it to the meetings at the Pen Club. They are located close by and he sees old friends there. Allen also attends War Resisters League meetings. He brings back elaborate doodles to be saved.

Allen works closely with Geoffrey Rips (*Freedom to Write Committee* staff) to edit a collection of recovered government documents. They concern covert FBI activities against organizations and individuals advocating social change. Allen contributes his own recovered documents. He also pens an introductory essay *Smoking Typewriters* that titles the book.

Allen Ginsberg Iran Crisis War Resisters League Cooper Union Great Hall meeting 10/23/90

———

The Naropa Poetry Wars is a regurgitation of the hubris of the late 1960s. In 1975, William S. Merwin and his fiancée, Dana Naone, ask a special dispensation of Chöygam Trungpa, Rinpoche. They want to attend his elite seminary in a remote location. Rinpoche consents. There is an uninhibited Halloween party in which ugly battles of will scandalously prevail!

In the bare power struggle, Rinpoche orders Merwin and his girlfriend to appear at an evening gathering, which they have refused to attend. Rinpoche has them forcibly summoned and stripped; the rest of the sangha is naked voluntarily. It is not an orgy but is still a strange event in which East beats West.

———

It is in the American grain to abhor political or artistic despotism.

———

Allen is relaxed with Tom and uses his primal mode of saying shocking things. Allen excuses Rinpoche's excesses by citing: Burroughs shooting Joan, Gregory's thieveries, and his own assumed abuses; Allen's point is that everyone goes over the top at least once. This is an example of a weak argument that Allen would delete.

Allen sniffs something is wrong. He is like a dog on a bone determined to dig up the truth. He is able to track rumors back to their sources to rebut an accusation. This dispute originates with Chöygam Trungpa Rinpoche's permission to poet W. S. Merwin and his girlfriend to attend Rinpoche's most advanced spiritual retreat. The retreat is usually reserved for only advanced practitioners. They are physically and emotionally mistreated. Allen is not there.

Allen gives an interview to Tom Clark for *The Boulder Monthly*. He trusts Tom's intelligence since the late 1960s. Tom is one of my favorite New York School poets. His *Paris Review* interview with Allen is particularly important to both Allen and Tom. Tom promises to let Allen edit the new interview before publication. However Tom edits the interview. Rushes it to press without Allen's consent. Clark edits Allen's comments to be especially damaging to both Allen and Naropa.

The Vajra Guards are an honorific group of devotees who stand as sentries or ushers at religious events and practice flower arrangements.

——

Because I am aware of Allen's generosity and courtesy to interviewers, it hurts my sense of loyalty to bardic fair play. Allen always gets to read proofs before publication and Tom promises to provide them. The article is rushed to publication to preserve distortions that Allen would hone differently. Proofs are not a usual practice for journalists, but it is the long recognized privilege of Allen's. He is sure that he can shape it up later.

Tom Clark's subsequent book *The Great Naropa Poetry War* is directed against Buddhists and Allen. Tom pushes Ginsberg into fact-checking mode. One repeated accusation is that the Vajra Guards are seen marching in formation carrying M-16 rifles. Allen makes nightly phone calls to track down the source of the M-16 rumors. He records over a dozen long calls. After weeks of following leads he finds that the original witness had seen the guards marching with broomsticks. I am angry about Tom's rough journalistic tactics with Allen. I understand suspicions about eastern religions and cult leaders. A skeptical disdain for social groups is an element in the long held American transcendental preference for the individual. What disappoints me is that the discussion becomes one of smears and accusations. Allen apologizes to Rinpoche. Allen knows that he stirred up the pot. Rinpoche advises Allen. "Breathe in the poison. Breathe out the nectar."

6AM Bob – I went thru all the mail – here's a pile of work – wake me at 11 Allen

Allen's persona is available to youth of each decade. The secret is that *Howl* is an ever-ready liberator. It delights readers of every generation. The poet's mind is childlike in its appreciation of the world. So too is youth in love with love being new. Pound says that poetry is news that stays news.

October 1978 CBGB's Fire Benefit includes a joint set by Richard Hell and Elvis Costello. Allen reads *Don't Grow Old*, which has the line *Yes yr arm hair will turn gray?* Squashed into my side, a droopy short purple haired punk girl with a hefty safety pin stuck through her eyebrow is jolted out of downer distraction and blurts out, "Ugh!" Allen looks past the dark eyeliner, craggy safety pin eyebrows, and thrift store splendor and addresses the little Buddha just beyond.

R. Kraut

Late 1979. Ginsberg Inc. hires Helena Hughes as assistant. She is a mutual friend with all the poets. Helena is a practicing Buddhist. Her Sangha savvy is an asset for our office. For many years she works as a waitress at CBGB. Helena organizes the rare week of great punk bands interspersed by poets reading at the club. The door raises money for St Mark's Church's restoration after losing its roof to fire. All the Poetry Project poets read and so does visiting Andrei Voznesenski.

Men tend to fall head over heels in love with Helena. She is circumspect and holds them off with inscrutable indifference. Ted gives me a caution about Helena. "Don't touch her. If you walk by her and lay your hand on her shoulder you will have to do it every time you walk by." Helena helps with typing filing and the ever-needy catalog of audiotapes. I heed Ted's advice.

This is good advice about working with anybody. I should keep my hands to myself. I treasure Ted's mentorship. He shows me what a poet truly is. I think about his words and they don't mean much at first hearing. Later, I realize that every long-married human has an imagination that keeps true to the ideal of original love.

Allen loves his dreams and fills his nightly journal pages with them. He constantly lives on several planes at once. He is in touch with his dreams. I am least interested by his dream journals. Allen is a dream.

I try to keep the Allen World of Big Time Poetry out of my world of unknown young word slingers and vice versa. Our worlds begin to overlap. I have a terrifying predawn nightmare during a 1980 summer stay in Northern Wisconsin. The air around my bed

I usually don't like my dreams as they are primarily neurotic and frustrating. They cause me to wake up glad to be out of the dream, but occasionally I am rocked by a prescient message. In this case, I have a perfectly Gothic dilemma. What happens to me in my own picture? How can Tom's handsome face be so horrific that every hair on my body stands on end for hours?

My Hindu interest allows me to believe that there are simultaneous planes of reality. The reality of a dream can slide into the every day plane with great commotion.

Allen is happiest in offering a helping hand. I delight to aid him in this manner. I am entering a selfless phase in our relationship that lasts many years. I think not for myself and never for a moment do I ever feel that Allen owes me anything. Why would I? I am become Irwin. I cannot ask Allen to help me get a literary reputation. I am too proud. Allen doesn't need for me to be a star. As Allen notes, we're always in heaven. There is no greater success in Irwin's immediate future but to serve Allen.

is charged as if visited by lightning. The trees take on grotesque dark shapes in the growing light. I am shaken and bug-eyed for most of the day. The dream is simple. I am the bartender in a Wild West cowboy saloon. I turn around to see myself in the mirror. My face is changed. I now have the handsome face of Tom Carey. Poet songwriter Tom is a friend of ours in the St Mark's community. He is kin to a famous Hollywood family. His older brother Steve Carey is a terrific poet who lives on the Lower East Side. Tom is gay. He has cute shaggy blond locks. He is working for the poet James Schuyler. Tom helps Jimmy manage his daily tasks. Jimmy is somewhat infatuated with Tom. Tom is also very close to Ted and Alice. Often Ted gives Tom rare books or signed broadsides to take over to the booksellers for ready cash. 1981. Tom is suddenly without a place to stay. He asks me if he can sleep in the little room off the kitchen. I ask Allen's permission who naturally gives it. The little room is a guest room. It has a very narrow captain's bed with cabinets above. An upright piano is perpendicular to the bed. A four-drawer filing cabinet is jammed in. There is very little space to walk around. Usually the door is open and the keys of the piano smile into the kitchen. The filing cabinet stores Allen's journals and typescripts.

Allen is a persistent journal writer and has been so since childhood. He composes poems. Records dreams. Makes observations about his friends in each journal until it's filled. He is careful about dating them. Each journal goes through a three-part process at Allen Cottage Industry.

1.   Allen fills the journal by hand. Writes the start and end dates on the cover.
2.   An apprentice (usually at Naropa's Jack Kerouac School of Disembodied Poetics) types up the journal.
3.   Allen corrects and amends the typescript.

Each journal has its own folder in the file drawer. It contains the original journal. The original typescript. The amended typescript. But not every journal is typed yet. Nor is every typescript reviewed by Allen. Ah another project awaits Allen's eye and hand.

Tom stays in the little bedroom on and off for half a year. This doesn't raise suspicions as Tom is utterly charming and infectiously friendly. But suddenly Tom is gone. Leaves the Lower East Side. I hear that he is checked into rehab for heroin addiction.

I immediately hurry to the little bedroom. Check the journal drawer. They are gutted! I feel horrible about allowing Tom into the apartment. I consult Ted about where Tom sells books and journals. Three repositories for Tom's thieving emerge. Bob Wilson of the Phoenix bookshop on Jones Street. Brian Bailey's bookstore on Broadway. Andreas Brown at 47th Street's Gotham Book Mart. Tom sells items from Ted Berrigan. James Schuyler. Now Allen. The book dealers assume Tom is sleeping with Allen.

Allen is very upset by the losses. He jumps into a cab to the Phoenix. Talks to Bob Wilson. Bob sweetly says "Allen go back there and take anything that is yours." Allen comes back with a modest stack of various sized notebooks. Brian Bailey and

———

Allen needs thieves, as he cannot steal. A junkie steals to feed a habit. He has no moral composure and thus will not hesitate in the thievery. Allen is too dependent on his persona to acquire a drug habit; this would destroy his spiritual composure and his moral brand. Allen looks into a junkie's gnarled Buddha and sees stealing as the junky does. He weeps for their souls as they lift his books. Allen needs his junky friends to give him his holy work on Earth and to avoid sainthood.

He loves this work!. At this moment, LES Poets are reading and sharing the Swedish murder mysteries by Maj Sjöwall and Per Wahlöö. Ted is a glorious detective.

Tom is a clumsy asshole. He breaks my trust in a nightmare. Book dealers generally can't afford to always do the right thing. Ted is both the arsonist and the fireman. I am trading in on my naiveté. I don't ask Tom the right questions about why he needs the little bed. So all the bodhisattvas drive all blame to themselves.

Andreas Brown are much less forthcoming than Bob. They deny all knowledge of buying any Ginsberg journals when I call them. The next step is to catalog the losses. We hire Ted to come over to help with the effort. After searching out some workable pills Ted goes to the kitchen to catalog the journals. He works against an existent list of journals. This indicates which typescripts and corrected typescripts exist. Ted creates a list of the missing journals.

Tom recovers from his drug habit and comes back to make amends (step nine of the twelve). He tells us that he is aware of the fact that some journals were transcribed and some were not. Tom claims that he only took the ones that had been typed. But Ted's accounting indicates many journals that had never been typed are missing. Some of these are the earliest journals. They contain early accounts of Kerouac and Burroughs. Tom is in a tough spot and cannot explain this huge loss. He understands that he looks awfully guilty. Promises to help us in any way he can. Mopes out. Ted chain-smokes as he pores over the details of the missing journals. He struggles to discover a pattern or clue that helps us recover them. Brian Bailey never acknowledges buying any of Allen's journals. All the book dealers know that Allen doesn't need the money. They know he is adamant about keeping his archives intact.

Allen Tom and I hail a cab to 47th Street Gotham Bookmart. *Wise Men Fish Here* hangs over the door. We file into the narrow store. Find Andreas Brown behind the counter. He knows we are coming. Andreas denies buying anything of Allen's. Since he is Allen's agent for Ginsberg's archives at Columbia University he is supposed to resist temptation. Tom stands cinematically tall.

Argument: How to Free the Prisoner

Goes eye to eye with Andreas exclaims "Yes you did!" After a long pause Andreas demurs "Oh wait." He runs upstairs. Several minutes later he is back holding several Ginsberg journals. Allen has to buy them back. Tom promises to pay Allen back. Now only a few recent journals are still missing. A larger group without typescripts from decades earlier remains missing. We are stymied.

A season passes. Jason Shinder calls. He is one of Allen's former Naropa teaching assistants. In Boulder Jason types up letters between Allen and Jack Kerouac. Allen and Jason plan to edit a book of the two friends' correspondence. Jack's widow Stella is not ready to start any new projects. The idea is mothballed. During our chitchat I tell Jason about the mystery of the missing journals. He interjects "Oh you know I have some of Allen's journals. I borrowed them several years back to work on the Jack letters book!" The receiver drops from my hand as I run to get the list of still missing journals. Sure enough Jason has all the early ones. He borrows them. Neglects to leave notes in their folders. Jason brings them over. They are crossed off the list. The only journals that remain missing are ones Tom admits to. Each has a typescript. The lost journals match the ones that Tom claims he took to Bailey. We submit that list to a journal that catalogs stolen literary property for book collectors. These notebooks never come home. Tom diligently repays Allen the Gotham debt. **Ted Berrigan leaves this spoof on my desk:**

____

Stella Kerouac is smart to mothball Jack's posthumous work for several decades. After Jack's death, he, Allen, and William grow in cultural importance. By keeping his archives coherent, Allen is coloring-in his persona. These journals are bedrock to the collection. In 1948, Allen and Jack and William only have wool topcoats to keep them warm. Their intertwining lives create a dynamo that is beating on my fire escape as I sit, 2014, Bob Dylan sings about an angel, my wrinkling hands in soft Namaste before the Rosetta Stone on my black t-shirt.

———

Here is a Homage to Frankie for Allen and Brother Bill and an Esenin Book which I hope you'll put in Peter's room since Naked Rock Musicians are in the Kitchen and I can't go through there.

This A.M. I mailed a 200 page letter to the Academy of Dollars telling them that the inordinately voluble and brilliant poets Bob Rueben and Shotze Kraut are subsisting on Buffalo Grass and Mother's Milk and will soon die, thus causing the entire Lower East Side to grind to an artistic halt unless they send you $1,000.00 immediately.

I assured them that Francine Gray, Clayton Eshelman, and Jim Brodey's ex roommate would be glad to vouch for you and that Carl Rakosi, Harry Roskolenko, and Rudy Burckhardt would give Shelley a testimonial any time. (so would I) over

So I hope something happens. If it does, it would be in the next couple weeks and if it don't they will probably write me and say Bob & Shelley who??

See you when my next pill kicks in. yr humble and obedient servant.

Nelson Rockefeller

PS If they don't give you any money, sell this note to Bob Wilson for twenty-five cents!

(Ted) 1 P.M. Thurs. ? May 78

Bob —

← here is a Homage to Frankie for Allen from Brother Bill

and an Esenin Book which I hope you'll put in Peter's room since Naked Rock Musicians are in the Kitchen and I can't go through there.

This A.M. I mailed a 200 page letter to The Academy of Dollars telling them that the inordinately voluble and brilliant poets Bob Rueben and Shotze Kraut are subsisting on Buffalo Grass and Mother's Milk and will soon die, thus causing the entire Lower East Side to grind to an artistic halt unless they send you $1,000 immediately.

I assured them that Francine Gray, Clayton Eshelman and Jim Brodey's ex-roommate would be glad to vouch for you and that Carl Rakosi, Harry Roskolenko and Rudy Burckhardt would...

So, I hope something happens. If it does, it would be in the next couple of weeks, and if it don't they will probably write me and say Bob & Shelley who??

See you when my next pill kicks in.

Yr humble and obedient Svt.

Nelson Rockefeller

PS: If they don't give you any money, sell this note to Bob Wilson for twenty-five cents!

(Ted)
1:00 p.m.
Thurs.
? May 78

I'm blessed to be close to Allen in his later years. I am retracing those years in my own life. At times I feel Irwin's head in my hands when I need to hold up my brow. I know Allen's aural funny bone rigor in composing my own verse.

Rules for Argumentation:

1. Tone of voice is not arguable.
2. Any falsehood is a foolery that destroys the basis of valid arguments.
3. Do not use second hand news. This is only gossip and not worth more breath.
4. Corroborate each fact.
5. In academic debate, it is OK to box the opponent into a corner. But, if you are trying to correct behavior, there must be a correct path left open to the opponent to experience the required change of consciousness.

Allen's reading of political rags for pleasure stems from the underground press of the labor movements of his youth and the excitement of mixing forbidden words with denied rights. The magazines relax him for they are a part of his broad research. Poets deal out the ultimate nonfiction. Poetry is beauty and beauty is truth and the truth is not fiction.

Allen Ginsberg is completely formed by a Renaissance of accomplishments. He changes poetry. Enlightens minions of ordinary minds. Founds a university. Saves fellow writers in jail. Allen floats above our struggling on East 12th Street. The retrieval of the missing archival objects is a primary tenet of the Allen cottage industry. It is fodder for it nurtures his sense of accomplishment. If Allen is furious with Tom Carey or me he doesn't show it. His goal in creating a working office with several employees is to help ease suffering in the world.

The easing of suffering comes though gaining awareness. Sentience. Commitment to issues. Establishing facts with multiple sources prompts one to have the authority to do right. Be mindful of your goal. Never box an opponent into a corner with argument. Unless your goal is only the ego gratification of a final kill. Allen has a deep well of compassion. He feels deeply for the weak misfits of society. He sees corrupt machinations of mankind as a source of pain. All beings compensate for this pain through the use of compensatory drugs or mind-numbing newsfeeds.

Broadly addicted to political newsletters. Allen copiously reads *I.F. Stone Weekly. The Washington Monthly. Counter Spy. The Berkeley Barb. WIN.* And *The New York Times*. His keen eyes can reparse a story to find the inner unstated truth. Allen and brother Eugene often talk late into night to share insights about the truths and untruths in the news. Both boys grow up under Naomi's tutelage. They know that her paranoid hallucinations are present in the media that everyone experiences. Allen's favorite light reading (the reading done while on the toilet) is pamphlets and magazines concerning international spying and subterfuge.

May 30, 83

Dear Bob —
please Check up on our subscription to Counter-Spy and WIN. and add +pay for subscriptions for Burroughs. +Lucien Carr at their respective addresses.

AG

———

Candor is the key to motivating people.
Allen's aphorism "Candor ends paranoia,"
resonates deeply for me as the core element
for his idiot naïveté, which is smart and
disarming. The individual is open and there
is no secret agenda to create fear. The truth
allows one to take off his or her clothes
without shame. Welcome each person back
into the garden before temptation. This
openness to the world allows one to incul-
cate a new truth and new way of perceiving
the righteous path.

Allen is aware of his ego nature. He lets me take on my own initiatives while working at his desk. As members of *Artists Call Against Intervention* in Nicaragua Kimiko Hahn and I organize a poetry reading by Ernesto Cardenal. He is the Minister of Culture in the leftist Sandinista government. He is coming to New York to speak at the United Nations. There is no other way for him to get into the USA. Kimiko liaisons with political groups. I arrange the poetry venue at the Great Hall of the Cooper Union. Of course my wishes and Allen's dovetail. Allen does not take ownership for all that he sponsors. He shares power to advance cultural awareness.

The Cardenal reading is free. The 920-seater Great Hall is filled beyond capacity with hundreds of people outside pushing to get in. I see Shelley fighting with security guards. I am unable

Even though Allen is teaching me, I am learning from the performance of assigned tasks. I add new tasks and in a sense reshape Allen if only to make him seem larger. I do not think myself good at what I do but I feel that I am able. I am able to use nearness to Allen to attain the right venue for Cardenal's politically charged poetry. The good press on the reading spotlights U.S. government interference in Nicaragua. The political operatives appreciate my work more than I do.

to get there. Allen reads English translations for Cardenal. The audience goes wild. The Nicaraguan delegation is pleased. Afterwards they take me to dinner in a small Spanish restaurant in Greenwich Village to thank me for my hard work.

"Don't thank me. I would do it again." I say.

"No. We do thank you for your work."

"But this is what we do." I demur.

"We are thanking you for your work!"

"Oh!" Got it!

5 Bodhisattva Hello

FAKE TREASURES

last blinding snows slipping into dusk
winter two thirds behind
this belies the end of white winter
soft breeze through window frame bristles up my arm
street lamps diffuse yellow flakes inland
this winter brought a clear message
in a dream that startled me to restless wakening
I was moving into my new apartment
the very one that has been a working waking dream in my life
but it was also the upper floor of my mother's house
I had been given a Buddhist shrine with incense burner, dorje, bells,
     miniature tankas and mandala, a large tarnished bronze
     statue of the Buddha
I decided to move the shrine from the porch to a bedroom
I carried the shrine with all the pieces atop
as I placed it into its proper spot
the statue of Buddha split diagonally in two
and bright red, blue, yellow, green gems fell out in a great rush
they bounced all across the freshly sanded wood floorboards
I despaired instantly
I knew I would never be able to retrieve all these precious Buddha parts again
as I held my head a voice entered -- yes from above
a male voice like the narrator to a public TV documentary spoke
"These are the fake treasures."
I picked up one bright piece and realized it was plastic like a Lego
that the pieces of my struggles and goals are indeed colorful blocks
that the inside of my objectives is a deep glory of nothingness
I can play with till nothing stops me

Did you bring extra cassettes? What if your machine stops recording? Do you have back-up batteries? What other interviews of mine have you read? Have you carefully thought about what you want to ask?

The student wants to back out but doesn't know how. Allen uses the wild eye. Anger inflamed, he turns slightly sideways to pierce deeper with his look. Try to ignore the spittle dripping down his palsied right cheek. For a second, it seems he might explode all over you. But as your panic peeks, he softens and straightens his terrible bent.

ALLEN CONSIDERS THE INTERVIEW to be his personal art form. He demands that the interviewer come fully equipped. Fully prepared with original questions. He yells at them if they are not. Then Allen pulls out his own supplies. The interviewers tremble and persevere to a surprising end. Allen turns his direct gaze towards the Bodhisattva inside each of them. His deep look erases the surface concerns of the interviewer. Reduces the formality

————

Kerouac explains: *Bodhisattva, a great wise being or great wise angel. Dharma Bums*.

————

Allen's introduction to Buddhism comes from Jack Kerouac. Jack reads the sacred texts and shares them with Allen. He points out the way of the dharma to Allen without abandoning his Catholic faith.

————

Lawrence Ferlinghetti mentions that he sees Allen at parties sucking special knowledge out of each new acquaintance's head as if through a straw.

————

Ah, Allen is Ishmael taking his watch at the masthead. He meditates on the surface of the sea. He is so mesmerized that he only spies whales deep within himself; does not raise a call to chase them. His whales are Blake, who is his voice, and Whitman in whose pod he swims.

————

Listen to Allen's voice as he sings his tuning of William Blake's *On Another's Sorrow*. This true concern is the path of the bodhisattva:

> And can He who smiles on all
> Hear the wren with sorrows small,
> Hear the small bird's grief and care,
> Hear the woes that infants bear --
>
> And not sit beside the nest,
> Pouring pity in their breast,
> And not sit the cradle near,
> Weeping tear on infant's tear?

————

Three or four different people stop me on First Avenue or in St. Mark's Church and relay this very story.

between the renowned writer and the inexperienced questioner. The rapport is properly reset. Allen offers his deepest wisdoms for a much longer and deeper conversation than anticipated. The interviewers immediately relax. Express their smartest selves. They always leave glowing. Allen's greatest skill is that he learns to address the Bodhisattva that lies within every sentient being. **Allen tells me that each person has at least the germ of a future Bodhisattva somewhere within his or her person. It is Allen's practice to address that small realm in every person he meets.**

His skill originates from an ability to concentrate his vision into a laser beam that has an acute power to illuminate. In a crowded party most of the people want to chat him up. He looks into one person's eyes. Stays there and there alone. His eyes are large and brown. They have a soft watery quality. Looking into them is gazing into the sea. There are all colors and strange sea creatures. Imagine the ocean looking into you!

Allen bravely exposes his own vulnerabilities. Sees the soft centers in others. His farsightedness into a person is based on compassion. He bypasses the barriers of fear and prejudice and egotism. Locates the subtle vulnerable germ of consciousness we are all born into.

Years later I am told a recurrent story. People who only meet Allen on the street say the same thing. Each teller is imbued with a special glow as they relate their tale. "I am walking up the avenue and see Allen. I say 'Hi!' and he turns to me and says 'Hi!' It so moved me. I will never forget it!" I am puzzled about how the brevity of the meeting contrasts with the longevity of the affect. I soon realize what is happening after several iterations of the simple story. Allen turns and bows slightly to greet the burgeoning Bodhisattva deep within the friendly passerby's chest area. The simple moment of communication unspoken and non-physical shines like a small flame in the moonless night. It provides a path through the darkness. Once the path to the Bodhisattva is lit that little light shines towards eternity.

I read Chöygam Trungpa Rinpoche's book *The Bodhisattva Path of Wisdom and Compassion*. The path is to absorb blame for all reproaches. One walks a righteous path as in the eightfold path. Through osmosis I receive Bodhisattva training in Allen's employ. I own blame because I am big enough. I do not give in to petty bitterness and disappointment for I must face them. I stay loyal to my teacher for his teaching is a form of consciousness. My crude groping at learning creates a balm to ease the path even for those struggling without the blessings of teachers.

I see love through Allen's eyes. I am challenged to accept the tender and caring love between men. See the neighborhood though Allen's eyes and linger within his poems to experience his voice as my own vision. Vulnerability is the last great lesson of Allen's eyes. Gaze into Allen's eyes on the *Kaddish* vinyl record cover by Richard Avedon. Yes he loves Richard. He loves Peter. He loves the viewer. *Kaddish* creates the pathos of a twelve-year-old boy's utter trust and vulnerability while taking his loving but dangerously disturbed mother onto his slender shoulders.

Allen uses these skills over and over to solve conflicts. To teach meditation techniques. To tap into ideas and facts for poems. If pushed he can push back and tangle up an adversary's mind in short order. A good example is found in Ginsberg's *Spontaneous Mind*. The 1988 interview by John Lofton reveals Allen deflecting an aggressive hostile questioning. Allen also turns

———

Is this a straight path? Shelley is my changeable weather and my sons are ports that are their sailings alone. Allen is neither straight nor gay to me. I love him like a son unable to come out of a torment. Allen shows me how to honor my real father by taking on the blame I bear him. That I love women makes no difference. The path of the Bodhisattva is always straight in the sense that light travels straight and truth is straight tacking.

———

Howl is labeled as angry. Years of meditation later, Allen sublimates anger to actually being able to manipulate another's thoughts without them being aware. Allen uses his power to win over and bring opponents together.

Mr. Lofton's moral indignation at Allen's sexual desires around. Elicits Lofton's own complex sexual fantasy:

AG: I should say my sexual preference is not exclusively for young boys but also for middle-aged men, straight men, and women. I've occasionally had fantasies about making out with trucks as well as beasts. And maybe I'll be making out with you before it's all over. (laughs)

JL: Well . . . maybe I'd like to drive the truck while you made out with it. If you don't mind an 18-wheeler with the pedal-to-the-metal.

AG: Well now here we are with . . . there's your fantasy! (laughs)

JL: Excuse me. You raised the idea of having sex with a truck.

AG: You extended it.

(Spontaneous Mind)

Allen does not compartmentalize his consciousness. His Buddhist immersions surface in all areas of his broad concerns. Buddhism does not teach one to misuse the x-ray powers of compassion. The problem with being a modern human is that one cannot avoid ego-tripping over one's own powers. Thus Allen is hard to argue with. In the late 1980s I put myself to a test. I am toying with the idea of leaving Allen's employ to apply for the director job at the Poetry Project. Eileen Myles is also in consideration. I talk to Allen about the job. He swings to me in his chair. Tells me that Eileen Myles is a much better poet than me. I am cut and deflated. I lose my willpower. I do not put in for the new job. I stay with Allen. This is the only goal of his crack at me. His mind gropes me. Leeches out my hidden doubt. Turns it on me. Depressed I carry on. I am slow to let it go.

———
Allen says, "young boys," instead of "young men," to broaden the impact and create a more flexible understanding of age of consent. It is provocative both overtly and subtly to enable the interviewer to expand his own perspective.

———
Have I been with Allen too long? Am I ruining my own writing career? Do I need to break from Allen?

———
Allen does not know my poems. But he knows my insecurity.

———
I do resent it. I feel helpless. I ruminate about my mean self-regard.

———

Allen consistently incorporates his sacred concepts into doodling while signing books for readers and friends. The skull with flower is one of Allen's oldest references. I imagine it dates to his early trips to Mexico and Day of the Dead celebrations. He always mixes his stars between five pointed and six pointed. He includes the mantra "AH" in the Buddha's lap; this mantra causes people to read it as initials. Allen describes AH as the utterance of wonder as first seeing fireworks in the sky. He champions the use of "OM" at political rallies until Trungpa Rinpoche tells him that "AH" is better;. "OM" is closed off at the end of its breath and "AH" is open-ended. Occasionally the office is asked if the initials stand for Adolf Hitler. Allen always puts the number "108" next to the Mala beads on the Buddha's arm. "108" is the number of mala beads and repetitions in the practice.

———

Let contradictions prevail!
Let one thing contradict an-
other! and let one line of my
poems contradict another!
Whitman *Respondez*

———

How can one judge another's practice? Is it the number of prostrations? Allen only does a fraction of the 100,000 required. On the other hand, he is recognized by his Gurus and does advance spiritually without displaying all the outer vestiges of religious practice.

———

I am interested in Buddhism but not sufficiently motivated enough to become Buddhist. Allen refers to me as a Jew. I am confused – isn't he as much a Jew as I? When a galley of a new David Meltzer book on Kabbalah comes in, he hands it to me and says, "Here, you are the Jew." But he is right. In my own life, I am slowly becoming Jewish although it seems to have little to do with Allen, whose practical philosophies of Buddhism fail to alter my heart. In the mid-1980s, Shelley and I send Aliah to Hebrew School at the Town and Village Synagogue on 14th Street. I walk into a Shabbat evening service and hear the tribal mutterings and singing in a language I seem to cleave to and instantly love. With my dysgraphia, I hear the sounds before seeing the words. I begin my Jewish practice, and I live a life based on Buddhist acceptance.

Allen does some sitting meditation every day. He does not seem to be a very committed practitioner but is unswerving over time. He is dedicated to spreading the Buddhist truths. Does so in his songs. *Do the Meditation. Gospel Noble Truths. Father Death Blues.*

I am working at the big desk in the front room. Allen comes home with a young man in tow. Indicating his bedroom Allen says "I am going to teach him how to meditate!" I smile. I think I know everything. I am sure it is a sexual tryst. Later I inquire of these men directly. Discover that Allen actually is teaching meditation. He doesn't neglect his enlightened mission. Later Allen may inquire. "Want to play some?"

In New York City Allen helps organize silent sitting sessions during large nuclear disarmament rallies at the United Nations.

We sit for hours. Finally my yoga kicks in as Allen keeps time. Rings a bell when it is time to stretch. Walk around. It is powerful to sit in a group sharing a collective consciousness on the mega ton problem of our age.

Working in the Buddhist community brings up the twin specters of egotism and incompetence. The Naropa Institute is the proving ground for young Buddhist workers. The staff is replaced each year. Every year I have to train new workers in the poetics department. Jacqueline Gens is in Boulder fighting the good fight for competency. She is a dedicated Buddhist practitioner. One of the few efficient administrators at Naropa. She calls most of the kids "airheads."

———
I act Buddhist at work, I do yoga at home, but I pray Jewish with my tribe.

———
Airhead replaces *idiot* as a Ginsberg word. Allen always has his ear close to the ground to pick up new twists on language that can be stored for possible future use.

3/5/85 Bob, [these are] not my glasses! I found mine (in my coat) finally. Sorry to trouble everyone
Airhead Ginsberg

Soon the budding Buddhist administrators become efficient. Then they move to higher Buddhist positions. Having to help the continuous stream of new workers makes me feel that Buddhism is passively coercive. They don't keep track of their archives. Allen makes tapes of classes. Gives them to Naropa. We also keep copies so we can copy them again as soon as Naropa loses them. Similarly we keep the posters and fliers to re-supply them. I teach new kids how to write press releases and business letters. How to handle cranky visiting poets.

1980. Allen engages me to help run the Summer Sessions. He pays me. I bring Shelley and our toddler Aliah. I am getting more skeptical about Buddhism. What is the point of disorganization and ego displays of temper? My work seems to be undone as soon as it is finished. Better to just party and not care.

A few weeks later. My family and I travel to New Mexico with Allen. Peter Orlovsky. Gregory Corso. I rent a big car and drive. I have dear cousins in Taos. Shelley and I hope to visit them. The big boys have a poetry reading in Santa Fe. Gregory is on his best and worst behavior. We visit a small homemade museum near the Spanish Peaks. It displays dusty artifacts of century old New Mexican life in foggy glass vitrines. Some antique silverware is displayed on tables. We get back to the car. Gregory opens his palm revealing a silver teaspoon he lifted. I know that Allen will get upset. Try to compel Gregory to take it back inside. Gregory will yell at Allen to mind his own business. Allen will then march back into the museum with the spoon. I am seduced by Gregory's confidence with me.

————
I am getting to be one smart airhead! I don't tell Allen.

Gregory, Shelley, Peter amusing two-year-old Aliah, and Bob on the road to New Mexico, 1980. Photo by AG

————

Memory ever shifts its episodic course through the oceans. Ishmael keeps track of time by inserting discourses, which are not novelistic.

I wonder why we stop here. The car is on the road. I assume that someone has to pee by a bush. Shelley is in a summer dress and flirting with Gregory. The sun is intense. Allen is not seen behind the lens. He has a broad straw sun hat. A shirt with his breast pocket occupied by several pens. His knobby legs wanly stick out beneath his Bermuda shorts. We are all being patient as he sets up his shot except for two year old Aliah who is enjoying the attention of the nearest adult. I am in the foreground attached to the car but relaxed in a falsely fey kind of pose. Perhaps my back aches. My camera is around my neck but my pictures are in my head. These are happy moments for everyone.

Allen is in the picture now; guess what he is holding. I bet Shelley has camera.

Men in grey suits politely yawn up their sleeves. Their wives are beautiful and dressed in suburban dresses. The children squirm in their seldom worn 'best' suits.

During this summer the 16th Gyalwa Karmapa Rangjung Rigpei Dorje comes to Boulder. There is much excitement. I attend his ceremony. In the large Dharma Hall I am reminded of the people I had seen as a child when I attend a Presbyterian service. The impressive colorful banners hanging on the walls make my foggy memories dissolve. Their primary colors sweep the WASP-like atmosphere away.

I stand in a line that approaches the seated Karmapa. He has a Tibetan club. He is bonking each person on the top of their heads as they bow to him. I figure it is a light tap like a dubbing. As I bow down to him he brings his arm down on me with force. All of a sudden everything goes black. I see white and blue stars circling my head like a halo. Dazedly I stumble away.

I am in an altered state for weeks after that. Sunny Broadway with its Chicago Hot Dog stand glows unseen by me before. I know that I am awakened in a subtle way. Nothing is changed except for having a feeling of change. But I do not have the gumption to ask the Buddhists what that is about.

Being a professional Buddhist means that I try to keep my prejudice and trivial angers out of the workplace. I read Yogi biographies in which Hindu saints call for spiritual detachment and the renunciation of material things. Allen exemplifies this. He gives away the things that have only material value but keeps the dear detritus of his closest friends and himself. Does he know there is gold in those things? Yes.

I start to understand Allen's investment in my family. He takes a great pride that I am able to raise and support a family with his meager wage. He never tells me so but I feel it every time he offers to raise my salary or brings me a gift from his travels. Buddhism means family and sangha to Allen. He comes to our crowded kid-friendly railroad flat on East 11th Street for Shelley's Hanukah potato latkes. He is like Uncle Scrooge joyously sharing a holiday meal with his clerk Bob. Allen makes life his family.

———

I don't even talk to Allen about it. I know that he would just smile at me in a knowing way.

———

I am a householder. I have a poetry father to obey and wife and sons to clothe, feed, and shelter. I also seek out an austere existence. I want to sit in Samadhi till my family grows up and leaves me. Ramakrishna clearly defines the householder's obligations. I must wait for my turn and meanwhile care for my family.

Allen Ginsberg & Bob Rosenthal Hanukah 1989. <u>A.G.</u> Rolliflex in Shelley's hands.

As I walk the streets of lower Manhattan, I remember to spread my hips, adjust my tailbone, lift out of the lower back and shine my chest up to greet each passersby. At first, I could remember once or twice a day to do mula bandha adjustment for only a few seconds. Slowly I increased the number of reminders to adjust. I remained adjusted for longer and longer.

My yoga practice aids my fledgling mindfulness training. Chronic lower back pains have plagued me since my youth. Doctors assure me that there is not much I can do about my poor posture and bent spine. After years of yoga lessons and mindfulness training my back does correct itself. The aura achieved by raising the glow of interconnected flowing spinal energy helps me to be a dharma worker. Helps me to spread the good karma of Allen Ginsberg.

I am starting to see myself as a Jewish-connected person.

The yoga connects the dots but the picture includes a minyan. I fumble through the prayers in English. The Hebrew chants are better. Indeed Hebrew is reputed to be the language of prayer. Here I am near midlife embarking into a spiritual realm with a vast tradition. My work with Allen gives me the courage to persevere. Begin to understand that it is the path to a spiritual renewal that is actually the destination.

Part of Allen's spiritual practice is to create a personal industriousness dedicated to furthering social change. Allen Ginsberg becomes a title he confers upon himself. He has created a persona. I am beginning to understand. Allen Ginsberg is bigger than just one human. Allen's birth name is Irwin Allen Ginsberg. I start to take note of the times I feel that I am only with Irwin. Usually that entails being in a place with no telephones such as a car trip. The "borrowed robes" of the bard slip off his shoulders and he relaxes in the front seat. He is a terrific map-reader. Gladly helps navigate. We can talk of anything and especially of nothing special.

Allen Ginsberg is a workaholic driven to succeed and achieve. He wants recognition for being benevolent. Irwin is a regular guy. A social being. Watching Allen be Allen is a pleasure. He does it so well. Stays in character all the time!

Allen has to create a forward-facing persona. His mother is too preoccupied by mental illness to mirror his infant expressions as most parents do. Allen has to create himself in his own mirror. He has to see a face that does not yet exist. He is isolated as a child. Has to invent his own love. His older brother Eugene is already burned out. Only dreams of escape. Louis his father endures his son's psychic need for physical contact. I can imagine

———

Shelley and I have Alice Notley and Allen over for dinner. There is French table wine and Shelley's excellent cooking. We chatter and gossip about friends for several hours. Irwin sits at the table languorously agitating with his Stim-u-dent, his shoulder bag hangs over the back of his chair. Allen looks up shocked and exclaims, "My God, we have wasted three hours!" Alice, Shelley and I keep giggling; Allen doesn't and makes his excuses to go as his hand fishes behind his chair for his shoulder bag. After Irwin leaves, we keep laughing.

———

As a nine year old he tells his diary that he would most likely be a genius writer. He isn't bragging; he is surviving. What choice does he have? In his household, he has to grow up fast.

———

As my sons are growing into rugged boys with tousled hair and toothy grins, Allen is becoming more tangible for me. We are sharing Irwin. I feel freer to touch Allen as Irwin might. A hand on his shoulder as I might place on my sons' backs as they sit doing homework.

I happen upon Allen making toast in the 12th street kitchen. One piece becomes stuck and starts to smoke. I see Allen approach the toaster with a fork poised above the smoking slot. I can't believe it; he proceeds to insert the fork into the toaster. I scream, "Allen, didn't you ever have a mother!" He looks up at me shocked with the fork hovering above the smoke. I walk over and unplug the toaster. "Now!" I say as if talking to a child. I am embarrassed. What a dumb thing to say! How accurate!

Louis girding himself as he allows his "love bug" younger son to cuddle with him in the night. Irwin once tells me that his homosexuality most likely came from his father not his mother. I am not sure what he means except I now guess it is about giving permission. Louis is in despair having a crazy wife Naomi. Later his patience is amply rewarded when he marries Edith.

In my imaginary view of Allen as a child he has a full beard and balding head. Yet the photographs show a sweet-faced big-eared lad whose large eyes already reflect the cares of the world. I start out a boundary setter in Allen's employ. I am on my way to becoming a disciple. I am in a fatherly place of balance.

6 Anger: Open Your Eyes!

from TO LIVE

most likely I'll just drown
in the swimming pool of anger
unrequited unmitigated unsupervised
anger gross in its approbation of expression
telling all near and far the redoubled meanings
the mishearing and twisting torture self inflicted
poor baby of fate
innocent harbinger of steam
foggy eyed truth seer
truth, truth, truth, truth
nothing to agree on
all I know now
is that my prayers were answered
I ended my Amidah praying
that God would let
anger unending
all dump onto me
not to hold back
once & forever
feel the cold to the marrow
trapped in every self made mirage
I still must learn to live

Anger is an arousal of ire.
Anger is a moment of thoughtlessness.
A centrifuge to extract
kindness and awareness
and drop them
into a murky pool.

"LET'S TAKE TURNS BEING ANGRY!" This unlikely statement is accurate. It is even more accurate to say "Let's take turns being stupid!" Anger seems to be a lifelong volleyball game for most people. *Howl* is often referred to as an angry poem. This is true that the angry god Moloch is in it. But this adventurous poem also speaks of compassion and solidarity. It defines a spot where people are stuck. Opens the door of self-realization to those who can hear it. Hearing has its own sense of direction. Allen's gravitational pull unites people. Geoffrey Chaucer's Prologue invites the reader to a pilgrimage. Charles Baudelaire opens the doors of the night. Reveals the flowers of darkness. Allen Ginsberg's visitations with William Blake and Walt Whitman offer a path beyond our inner strengths to a bonding concentration of community.

Howl is a liberating document. Its voice of kindness is a comforting madness. How do we stay calm in a world where mutually assured destruction is only a distraction? Allen overcomes with sensuality and provides a new moral compass to go forward. He parlays his sudden notoriety from *Howl* to focus his sacred love on his friends' novels. He rails against editors and publishers who shut their doors to them. Allen knows that his friends are great writers. To Kerouac Allen is pushy obnoxious red diaper Carlo Marx. He is ultimately successful in helping Burroughs to find print. Allen's anger is borne out of love. His meditative training through Buddhist practice mollifies the extent of his anger.

1978. Boulder Colorado. Allen wants to express anger again. He protests the work of the Rocky Flats Armament plant. It produces small fissile nuclear warheads that ignite larger fusion based bombs. He works closely with a local concerned citizens group called the Rocky Flats Truth Force. Allen composes *Plutonian Ode* the night before a planned civil disobedience. They sit on the railroad tracks to the plant to block a munitions shipment. He reads this first draft of the poem on the tracks. He and Peter Orlovsky are arrested along with Anne Waldman and others. This is a cause worthy of righteous anger. He wants to reach back and find that ancient angry God. *Howl* flows without hesitation. *Plu-*

tonian Ode relies on poetic tricks of conflagration. The anger is manufactured and academic. The poem is beautiful and the last section brilliantly links Walt Whitman to a future for poets to come. Allen has me send the poem to over thirty of his writer friends old and young to amend. Fix. Make suggestions.

Bob I have 3 extra copies of Plute Ode as is – filed <u>in left hand</u> drawer / Make a Couple of Copies of page 5 only <u>extra</u> / (PS shd be retyped sooner or later) – Allen

Who we need to send to? Send one to Nanda. one to Eric Elgharibli Paris

———

Jonathan shocks me. He is the boy in the *Emperor's New Clothes*. Allen is truly naive and impossible to outwit. I believe in Allen. I take his advice about anger to heart. I practice patience and generosity. This makes me secretly hostile. I slam the phone down after each call. I refuse to feel that working for Allen is just business. That is the point - it isn't just business. I hate people who steal from Allen because he has so little to steal. I can see how naked he is. Jonathan sees Allen as pathetic. Yet, he does give Allen his money's worth in Blakean poetic imagination.

Allen's young poet friend Jonathan Robbins reduces the 65-lined poem to ten or twelve lines. Allen is charmed but does not follow these changes. Jonathan is a handsome teenager. Haughty but not gay. Allen is head over heels in love with him. Allen allows Jonathan the use of his charge account at the Gotham Book Mart. I am shocked. Jonathan calls Allen a "creep." Beyond shock I am angry. Jonathan has run up over $300 in charges for books. Calls Allen an awful name! I mention this to Ted who thinks a moment. Turns his face to me. Ted says "You know

Allen is a creep but the important thing is that he is also Allen Ginsberg!" Ted's emphasis rises. The *Allen Ginsberg* at the end of the sentence sings out in the voice of the brand name Ginsberg.

One afternoon Jonathon calls me up. He wants someone to meet him at the Metropolitan Museum. I agree. Jonathan is very interested in ornate silver snuffboxes. I feel competitive with him. He is erudite and superior. I try to trump him when I tell him my father is a psychoanalyst. He turns to me and calmly wins the gambit by telling me "My mother is a psychoanalyst!" Shelley is pregnant. Jonathan chides me for bringing another human being into "this vile world." "With its silver snuffboxes!" I think.

Soon after there is a poets' party in Allen's apartment. Allen has made a large pot of soup and serves a large wedge of Gorgonzola. Jonathan is there. So is Shelley. Shelley shows hugely. She stands like a small mountain filling the narrow opening to Peter's bedroom. Jonathan resumes his criticism of our population growth. I glance across the crowded kitchen. I see her wedge him in with her body. Wag her strong pointer finger in his face. She hoots in annoyance as we walk home. "That little snot!"

Allen teaches us that anger can be greatly reduced by direct observation. Kerouac has a line of poetry in *Mexico City Blues* that Allen loves: *Anger doesn't like to be reminded of fits.* He allows his anger its full expression (yelling and pounding the desk with his fists). A lack of glue on his desk. A death-wish for old friends turned neo-cons like Norman Podhoretz. Yet it is clear he does bear his own hurts. When insulted he is very restrained. The angry person is always the one to suffer more. "Anger creates bad karma." As correct as it sounds I don't accept it yet. I am still angry with my father and my brother. I fight with Shelley. The

Psychoanalysis is a devotion to my parents. I seem to be its case study: *Little Oedipus*, Psychoneurotic, Learning Disabled, Pre-Schizophrenic, Unhappy!

———

People are such idiots. They are endlessly mean. It never changes. Cruelty is the coin of every realm. How could a thinking person deliberately choose to add to the misery on the planet?

———

Shelley embodies truth in anger. It is not important whether it is rightful or wrongful. Her truth is a constant. She confounds Jonathan.

———

Anger doesn't like to be reminded of fits. Anger circles itself. From the smallest pricking, it revs itself into a whirlwind. As it whirls around, it gets louder and louder "repeating itself" until it is nothing but noise and stupidity. Anger is a mind trap that can be released by objective seeing. Feel the anger, observe it, feel it subside and say something calm. One's overall effectiveness is vastly increased. Allen practices this successfully.

children frustrate me. Ronald Reagan's false compassion only makes me hate him more. I am bitter that I am not a better poet. God no I cling to my right to be angry. After all what else do I really have? Allen breaks me down in a direct and painful way.

The Kush Episode:

Over many years Allen amasses hundreds of tapes of his poetry readings. In the 1960s Barry Miles is hired to listen to the tapes. To create an audio *Best of* Allen's readings. Fantasy Records is going to produce it. Miles assembles a new master by splicing out the good readings. Adds them to master reels. The project falls through. The thought of producing a record album fades over time. The master tapes languish in Fantasy's storage vault.

In the 1980s Hal Willner is making a compilation of Allen's best readings. Allen pays Fantasy Records to retrieve the tapes. They send several boxes of reel-to-reel tapes to Allen care of City Lights Bookstore. Allen is in San Francisco and at City Lights when the boxes arrive. Allen is trying to get to the airport. He has no idea what to do with the boxes. As fate would have it Kush shows up at City Lights as Allen stands on Columbus Avenue pondering his new dilemma.

"Let me hold them for you Allen." Kush pipes up "I will treat them well. Catalog what is on them." Allen is happy. "Great! I'll pay you to make cassette copies for me so I can listen to them myself." Hal Willner is slowly working on the recording project and does not need the Fantasy material at the beginning. Kush is strangely resistant when Hal does contact Kush to pick up the tapes. Hal asks me to intercede.

I call Kush. He explains that he has taken excellent care of the tapes. "You never made cassettes for Allen," I remind him. "Well," he answers. "You see I have been hard at work winding the tapes by hand. These old audiotapes get a lot of audio bleeds when they sit idle for long periods of time. They need to be slowly and gently wound and rewound by hand!" "But Kush all we asked for were cassettes." "I was afraid to play them until I had established their integrity. I have been hand winding them for many months already." "Gee Kush you should have checked with us before you did all that." "You don't understand. These tapes are valuable and must be hand wound!" "How many hours have you logged doing this?" " 125 hours." "How much will that cost?" "$25,000." "But Kush. This is unfair! We never agreed to that expense. We only wanted a set of cassettes!" "Hand winding is the best and only way to save these tapes." "Let me think about this." "I can't give Willner the tapes until I have been paid!" "What! You are holding them ransom for payment when you never asked if you could undertake that part of the job. Nor did you ever invoice us!?" The large price of his work must have made Kush afraid to invoice Allen. Or even inform us that he is creating a large bill. Now I am livid. "Kush nobody in my experience has treated Allen as badly as you are doing now!"

I slam down the phone hanging up on him.

Kush is a workaholic like Allen. Kush adores Allen the way Starbuck adores Ahab and must do what he knows to be right. The whale is the solution. There is a living wound in Starbuck who misses the profits paid out to retrieve the poetry tapes!

I am seething and hardly able to breath. I contact Allen. Tell him the entire story including my angry hang up. Allen empathically says "Oh no! Anger will produce bad karma and make things worse. I better call Kush quickly!" I don't want Allen to cut me out. This would destroy my working relationship with him. I am protecting my position as right hand man. I would be locked out of the castle if Allen goes around me. I immediately declare "No Allen, please let me do this. I will call him back and work it out." Allen (I hear him smiling) agrees.

I call Kush back to let him know that I want to negotiate a reduced price for the hand winding. Kush is dug in on the amount and won't budge. By coincidence a recording engineer from the Smithsonian calls Allen Inc. I use this opportunity to discuss the worth of hand winding old tapes. He is shocked and says it is absolutely unnecessary and useless to hand wind tapes. This makes me even angrier. I tell Kush what the Smithsonian said but he does not care. The stalemate is broken by Kush telling me that I have to speak to his representative in Chicago. Allen doesn't even have $25,000 in hand. I call the representative in Chicago as requested. We talk and argue. He has no knowledge of audio engineering. I wonder what his role is. I decide to continue to play hardball with the new player. Finally he cracks. Admits that Kush is his son-in-law. "Oh!" I think suddenly deflated. "Here is a father whose daughter marries a quirky poverty stricken soundman!" The Chicago father-in-law pleads with us to pay them off. Let Kush have his first nest egg. A father myself, I know when I am defeated. Allen pays the entire amount in installments. Willner gets the tapes. The money means nothing to Allen. It means everything to me the workingman. I agree that hanging up on Kush is a huge mistake as it ruins any chance of a reduced settlement. Allen is right. My anger does produce bad karma.

Where do I go wrong? I am not wrong. But anger makes me wrong. I go from *in the right* to *in the wrong*. I practice tolerance. Try hard to be aware of my own anger. Parents need limitless patience. Experts advise new parents that children eventually will break everything. It hurts much less if one understands that. With Kush my anger is magnified by my allegiance to Allen. Hurt me and I get it but *hurt my family that's different.* In *Kill Your Darlings* a recent movie about Allen the screenwriter has Louis slap young Allen across the face for being rude to Edith. I am

———

I don't hate Kush. Allen pays for me to learn the lesson of the cuckolded husband. He who discovers his wife in bed with the neighbor but only sees a mule, as she claims, is a wise man.

———

There is no cost to breaking everything. The sense of loss however can feel acute.

Pains of unknown origin inhabit the tears spent over a smashed ceramic bowl. I realize that I express anger to my kids. If the two-year-old kid breaks grip, runs off the curb into traffic, allow a swat behind and then what? I set the course to stopping generational violence. My father hit me for not eating dinner fast enough. Now I am fat. I do not want my children to carry my burden when they are adults.

stung by this slap on every level. Allen is never rude to Edith. Louis and Allen are long correspondents. They know how to express all their feelings. This untruthful scene hurts Eugene's and Edith's children. Allen does not counter violence with violence. He offers soup and LSD. He bows to the inner self. It is too late to hold on to anger after counting to ten.

Peter Orlovsky is a lovely person. He is eccentric and sweet to me. Peter is a big child. I love his compassionate transparent poetry. His enthusiasm is infectious. However after his poetry book publication he starts to grow dark. He begins to stay shut up in his bedroom for days on end. I don't think much of it until Allen takes me aside. Whispers "I found out what Peter is doing in there. He's drinking!" I am surprised at Peter then but later I am more surprised at Allen for feigning surprise himself.

Peter seems to be on an emotional downward spiral. He has a coke dealer living at Committee Farm who cuts down trees for cash. Runs up a bill of several thousand dollars on phone calls to Hawaii. Peter relinquishes management of the farm. His blue Volvo station wagon amasses a mountain of parking tickets. It has to be gotten rid of. As the responsibility for Peter's life deserts Peter it falls to me. I intercede on the farm bills. I get the parking tickets paid. The car is towed off. Peter is getting more erratic and manic. Compulsive behaviors appear such as repeatedly offering to cut my hair. Drinking his first piss of the morning.

I lose my perspective. I am inured to the reality of Peter's mental distress and pain. I am feeling closer and closer to Peter. If I have to do diapers I want to help him potty train. I trust in his true regard for me.

I decide that I need to learn how to "let go" of someone.

Allen welcomes my willingness to work with Peter. Whereas Allen usually is a confederate with Peter's girlfriends, my allegiance is to Allen who is in Boulder most of the time. Peter's daily ups and downs are my responsibility.

Peter might be able to manage a family and job. But it would have to have been in the early 1960s. Instead, Peter becomes a poet / songwriter, which opens him up to deep, gothic fears and gross imbalances. In *Message*, Allen vows to accept Peter and his brothers' mad cases. Peter becomes the medieval fool poet who cries through his motley.

Helena Hughes should move on. She has finished a big project. We don't need the extra help. I try to ease her out of her employment in a way that seems natural and not a dismissal. She is too smart for my clumsy efforts. She goes to Allen and talks up all her sangha connections. Allen urges me to keep her on. I learn that I should bring Allen into my schemes especially when it comes to "letting people go." Helena leaves on her own accord to work for James Schuyler in the Hotel Chelsea.

Early 1984. Juanita Lieberman starts to work for us. She is young. Conscientious worker. Fluent in English Spanish and French. She is also Peter's girlfriend. Juanita is holding Peter together. They set up housekeeping in the adjacent apartment (number twenty-four). Even with Juanita's love Peter continues to decline. I hear a lot about it from Juanita. Peter harasses her at times. At other times he is hopelessly full of remorse. The situation is a difficult one for Allen. Allen loves Peter. Does not begrudge him girlfriends as long as he (Allen) is somehow in the mix. Juanita works for Allen. Peter needs money from Allen. Allen is still secure in that he feeds everyone.

Allen keeps a filing cabinet with information on Peter's health and treatments. With every new psychic disturbance Allen runs to see the new doctors. He tries to impress upon them which medications have worked and which have not. He keeps handwritten notes. Makes copies of reports. The files bulk up over time. Peter's ups and downs thrill Allen. It connects him to family and security. It is Allen's way of "being in control." I grow inured to Allen's excitement. I am enlisted into the Peter Orlovsky emergency squad. Call doctors and nurses. Arrange for Peter to receive his medication. Pick up his vitamins. I expect the

Juanita loves Peter and seems to fit into all of our lives. She sides with Peter when it comes to Peter. She sides with Allen when it comes to me. She sides with me when it comes to life and limb.

It takes the most extreme conditions to make Allen feel secure. Yes, he is controlling and yes he is concerned for Peter, but when Peter is on his worst behavior, Allen looks larger than life, agitated, and excited as a kid on Christmas morning.

extreme at work. I come home to the calming chaos of two kids and frazzled mom.

Juanita wants Peter to break away from Allen. Become independent. She holds out on the possibility of marriage and children for Peter. This year Allen has a four-month trip to China scheduled. As soon as he leaves things on 12th Street quickly go from bad to worse.

Peter is drunk all the time. He comes into the office to annoy me. Take up my time. Juanita and I lock him out. He comes over on the fire escape. We lock the windows. He stays on the fire escape rapping on the windows. There is more than one occasion when I have to sneak Juanita out of the building for her own safety. I hide her one block away in my apartment. Peter has his father's machete. He marches around with it. I still feel no fear of Peter. I love him.

The situation worsens until no work can get done. All of our time is concentrated on Peter. Is he here? Is he on the fire escape? Is he sober? Is he coherent? Is the machete in his hand? Less than a week after the Bumpers Case Peter builds up to his own breakdown.

The sky falls. Peter strikes at my crotch with scissors. I feel its point go through my jeans. Dimple the skin of my scrotum. Peter shoves his beet red face bulging veins into my face. Screams at the top of his lungs. I feel my love for Peter drain from the top of my head down through my legs. Out my toes. Like stomping on an open tube of toothpaste. Peter drives my love for him out of me. I have never experienced a rupture such as this before.

My unreserved love for Peter dies. So does the romantic

———

October 29, 1984, there is a terrible police incident in the Bronx. A woman, named Eleanor Bumpers, has been given an eviction notice. She refuses to leave. The police are called. In their struggle to force her out of her own door, police shoot Bumpers to death with a 12-gauge shotgun. The media go nuts. The police are under close scrutiny now.

———

"I am going to sodomize your children!"

I warn my small sons to never go near Peter again. Later, I order both of them to cross the street if they see Peter at a distance. The Buddhists have a phrase, idiot compassion; I am their top model. I risk my life on love.

—

It takes me five single-spaced typed pages to explain the entire incident to Allen. Yet, I cannot share a truth with Allen that is compellingly short and simple for me: **I lose my love for Peter.** The most important detail to me is left out. Peter's threat is so horrible that I unconsciously cannot bear to add it to my letter.

—

After this incident, I walk around New York City bent over with woe. Shelley grabs me and orders me to start yoga immediately. I go to our dancer friend, Ellen Saltonstall, a gifted yoga teacher, and start a twenty-year practice that cures my aching back!

veneer. A more sober and saddened version of myself can be civil to Peter after this. Our relations are now detached and business-like. Neither his pain nor his health are of my primary concern anymore.

I send a telegram to Allen at Fudan University in Shanghai. A few days later I write a long detailed account of exactly what happened. I include it here without much normalization of punctuation or tense. At the end of the letter I feel entitled to add my own thoughts about what would be good for both Allen and Peter and Juanita and myself.

12 5 84

```
NNNN
1356

ZCZC DK2755 FD9961 GRX449 RGB1960
SHDK BB SHDF
CNSH CO URDB 021
NEWYORKNY 21/19 29 2217

ALLEN GINSBERG
FOREIGN LANGUAGE DEPARTMENT,
FUDAN UNIVERSITY
SHANGHAI

ATTENTION MR. CHENG YUMIN,
PETER IN BELLVUE PSYCH. CALL IMMEDIATELY
                              BOB

COL DEPARTMENT, MR. YUMIN, PSYCH.
```

```
NNNNX
0352

ZCZC DK3832 FD1165 DF5132 FD1154
SHDK BB SHDF
```

Dear Allen,

OK I don't know exactly what shape this letter will take since there is so much that I would like to convey. First, I am not seeing Peter today but I saw him yesterday given a special quiet room to do it so he has gomden, zabuton, beads, watch, picture and all to enable him to get started on his mantras. He is slowly coming around to recognizing his problems and besides begging forgiveness has in fact mentioned that perhaps an in-hospital stay just for alcohol abuse at the VA may be a good transition before coming home. Perhaps this will not happen but it indicates that PO [Peter Orlovsky] is starting to grasp the seriousness of his condition besides saying what we all want to hear. PO slowly dropping demands for speedy release further indication of acceptance of need of help. Now I will backtrack as best I can. You remember the rages that PO spilled out while you were still in California well as soon as you left for china he calmed down although he and I did have a clear talk about ourselves just prior to his cooling out. He was going on and on about Miles [Barry Miles] in this case as an illustration of your stupidity. i.e. you allow someone to make $100,000. and take nothing for yourself. And I explained that in many ways I really agree with him (not so much about Miles because you did help Morgan [Bill Morgan]) and I used the example of copying the Beat Generation lectures at Naropa for your own archive, spending 300+ on a machine, paying Randy [Roark] and buying tapes in all spending about 1500. and who gets the tapes when they come in – Miles who is getting more to write a bio of you than you will on your own lifework so why can't well paid biographer travel to Boulder where originals are held OK I say to PO listen I am not a James Grauerholtz [William Burroughs's secretary] I don't want to control AG [Allen Ginsberg] life and $ and besides I don't get enough $ to want to do so in order to keep my own life clear and unconfused I let AG do as much as he please in ways that don't please me etc. PO seemed to recognize that I am not AG extension or surrogate OK so PO calmed down and left me alone at work and no longer demanded giant reading tours and just left me alone but did booze plenty often when I saw him he reeked of foul hair tonic and sake breath. So I write to AG that PO is ok and letting me be etc. The next incident occurred on Nov. 8 at apt. 23 where I had arranged a tenants meeting and a member of GOLES to attend. Crowded kitchen with Goles guy and everybody has lots of questions and George [the super] is upset because he is fired and threatened his eviction etc. Peter brought a big bottle of scotch and kept trying to get people to have a drink and when rent strike was suggested to counter the landlord moves peter argues against it in an irrational manner, refusing to listen to others or letting others even talk. Everyone tried to shut him up and JL [Juanita Lieberman] was mortified. PO was in a sense forbidden to attend the next meeting. JL and PO had a huge fight that night, broken dishes etc. and then PO apologized and got back on track (still drinking) he took care of his court related matters and registered to vote here and transferred the car registration address to the street address and although drunk was not oppressing me. Once he did make me write a letter to you which PO dictated and it went on and on about you and the Tibetan Wife and baby later that day he asked for the letter and ripped it up. The farm became a problem since that guy there left surely sticking COP with giant phone bills and no one there to watch the place. PO went to Karme Chöing around Thanksgiving. He was supposed to go the farm but didn't. He came back from karma Chöling on Nov. 26,

Good Old Lower East Side local housing rights organization.

The farm is the property upstate. Maybe the build up to this melt down starts there?

Mon. Gordon Ball was staying here and showed films at MOMA that night. He and PO talked long talk that night. Tuesday PO went to see his mommy. We didn't know this then but he told us later that he brought booze with him and acted badly, "played with knives", ripped up a $20. smock he had given to Marie [PO's sister]. He upset them very much and when he returned to the city Tues. night he told JL that it was lucky he was alive he had driven at high speeds drunk. Wed. was still grim. PO hardly talking just glaring. JL said he was not sleeping and he kept her up all night while she tried to ignore him and pretend to sleep. Coffee/sake/coffee/sake . . . Ira Lowe [AG's lawyer] came over to see office Wed. morning. PO greets him and offers to cut his hair. (PO had bought fancy hair scissors) Ira declines offer and wants PO to really talk to him PO gets scissors [our] meeting with Ira disturbed repeatedly. Ira leaves sooner than planned. PO sez later that he must buy a typewriter for his mommy she needs it must have it now etc. I phone place find out cost and tell him where to go. He goes out to buy typewriter. JL and I work. Thurs. Nov 29, PO starts as soon as I come in with a demand (repeated from day before) that I set him and JL on a 20 million dollar reading tour, over and over. Miles comes over to do some work. PO berates him, brings him guitars, offers haircut shows scissors then standing among Miles, JL, and myself PO runs scissors through his own hair (in office) slipping fall to desk and floor. "Oh Peter no No," we say. Miles leaves. (actually there is still hair in the typewriter I can't get it all out of here) JL very upset – crying? PO flicks scissors against his skin oh yes he has been naked for two days. I decide that today is the day that something happens. Hair cutting is oldest, clearest, sign of crazy plea for help. PO eyes pinpoints of anguish, red face, veins bulging, screaming about twenty million. I called my cousin Larry [Siever] who works at Bronx VA he is a psychiatrist and I had talked about the PO situation before. I got Larry and told him that the matter we had discussed before was now holding scissors up to me. (he had the butcher knife between his legs under his cock) Larry understood and told me that I had two choices 1. walk him into VA [Manhattan] 2. call cops for ride to Bellevue. I called the VA and they said just bring him in. I asked PO if he would walk up to VA with me and he said sure. JL got his pants and shirt. PO refused to put them on the more I tried to get them on the more he became hostile to me. Put the butcher knife up to my neck and threatened to cut my head off (oh yes Bill Morgan had come by sat silent strong behind me) PO refused clothes and was still cutting his hair. I called 9th precinct and got civilian operator who encouraged me to once more try to get PO voluntary to hospital "They don't like the uniform" she said. I try again to get PO in pants. Frenzied father forcing deranged child into pants. The scissors are more and more pointed or brought close to my neck. I redial the precinct and PO pushed the button on the phone. I am afraid to get into a physical fight with PO, knife, and phone. I rush out knocking on doors—no one is home! I sneak back into your room and call police. I tell them, friend is crazy, threatening me with butcher knife and scissors. They are on their way. I come out into the kitchen and meet PO who is asking Bill Morgan to go out and get another bottle of sake. Bill agrees but on way out I ask BM [Bill Morgan] to watch front doors for police. Meanwhile PO and I still argue about him going voluntary. I did not tell him that I had called the police but he must have known I was trying. I hold the pants up "Just the pants Peter, it's not too late." PO takes scissors, point extended half inch out of fist and full force, red face bulging veins slams the scissors into my crotch. He pulls back and does not actually stick me but I feel point come against my genitals. I

Sniping one's own hair with stabbing gestures revs up the whirlwind of violence.

am stunned, then turn and walk out, run downstairs to be with BM at door getting my breath. I say that I am going to go up and stay in the hallway till cops come. I go up and there is PO in hallway trying to get into his own door. can't manage the key drops it, gives up goes back into 23 kitchen. I wonder where JL is and carefully enter 23 apt. and can't find her. I start yelling for JL and she comes out of her apt. she had fled PO and locked him out with extra latch on door (you know it) I forget what had happened then why she fled but next thing was the arrival of the first two officers. I meet them in the hall and tell them about PO and bring them in. They first see PO, naked in kitchen holding scissors, hair deranged. They say, "Peter would you like to come with us?" "Why sure officer, just let me get some clothes." I say I have them right here in the office but PO leads officers to 24 apt. and quickly slips in and shuts door adding extra latch. Police call for more [police]. It is now about 4:30 PM. The police will not force the door. Recently cops shot and killed a black lady they were evicting in the Bronx big stir) cops being extra careful. High ranking cops come. JL sez they can get [in] through the fire escape the window was open. She leads two cops to bathtub [fire escape window above it] and just has the window open when head cop in hallway tells me to fetch those guys back so I do and that leaves JL on her way out the fire escape alone. She goes next door and finds PO in the living room dressed in a suit. He tells her to tell the police to go away. She tells him that he has to tell them and he says "no no no you do it." She goes back out via fire escape and talks to cops. Now cops put man on window on fire escape and no one can go in or out that window. Cops call hostage negotiation team. I go out on fire escape and yell into Peter and try to persuade him. He does not respond. I ask [{the officer} if I can go in and the answer is negative. I try phoning he doesn't answer. Micheal Brownstein comes out of his apt. acts imperious and demands to know what gives. He offers to talk to PO. JL lets him have it. She tells MB [Michael Brownstein] that he doesn't really care and to leave them alone. What could he do? I was glad to see MB backed off but did remember that perhaps PO would listen to Buddhist. We had called David Rome earlier but he was in a meeting and never called back. JL called him and got him out of the meeting but I talked to him and he agreed to call Marvin Moore to come over. Police were happy to wait. I asked MB to call Dharmadhatu (something to do) then he went downstairs to wait for Marvin. MB told BM that we should not have called the "pigs" why hadn't we called him first. Marvin arrived about 5:15 and chief hostage negotiator arrived we powwowed in office here. I filled everyone in. I had described PO at least ten times to each new chain of command and was feeling crazed myself. Police littered the entire house, sitting around, reading books, discussing their code names for that shift. Channel nine tv news was waiting on the street and the whole neighborhood was out there and in the hallway. Marvin went to the door flanked with the chief negotiator. He called to PO and PO responded and talked. Marvin mentioned some eight fold path stuff and finally asked PO if there was anything he could get him. PO wanted a cup of coffee and a bottle of sake. The police agreed to the sake. PO spelled out where the liquor store was and slipped first a $100 bill then a second and then a ten for the sake. The police went out and got the sake. There were police with giant tranquilizing guns, big padded forks to trap a person against the wall, and guys outside across the street further watching the window. Marvin told PO that the sake was there and asked him to undo the latch and further told PO that there would be a lot of action when he did unlatch the

———
Dharmadhatu becomes Shambhala.

door. PO unlatched the door and walked back to the center of his apt. Marven opened the door followed by police. PO was naked and completely shorn of hair. JL went in. As police handcuffed PO he said, "you know you don't need to put these on." But there's no more time for PO to put his pants on. They brought up a giant metal chair on wheels and gently put PO into the chair, wrapped him in a sheet, and strapped him in. JL screamed at the police, 'you get your kicks doing this . . .' Finally officer, detective in brown wool trench coat, said next time don't call us. They hoisted PO in chair and carried him down the stairs he howled and crazy laughed all the way. JL and Marvin and I collected clothes and I put a copy of <u>Clean Asshole Poems</u> in my pocket. With all the surreal attraction of drunk street people and neighbors and PO in high chair under tv lights he is placed in ambulance. Marvin and JL go with PO and I was to follow in a squad car. Cops never jerked or twisted or hurt PO. Nice cop one of the first on the scene told me to calm JL down. He gave me time to do that I told her not to come down on police. In ambulance PO turned to black cop (the one JL feel least sympathy from) and sez, "How much you make?" Cop says "None of your business, I know your type, you always end up this way!" PO screams loud in little ambulance, cop screams right back, JL is afraid PO will get punched out. Marvin now responding [alert] probably never heard PO yell loud before. JL snaps at cop, "this reflects on [you], this guy is going to Bellevue!" and cop calms down and without further provocation all arrive at Bellevue. Once in Bellevue PO is just another deranged patient --it is a little after 6:00 PM. PO is after some delays released from cuffs and we give him his robe and [he] is put on bed with a single safety strap. PO very depressed very very very unhappy. Immediately wants us to get Joe Gross get Eugene get him out. PO sitting up cross-legged in tiny room off main waiting, staging areas for this not craziness. After waiting hours we see doctor, this doctor merely to decide if PO in two days or out now. I show doctor PO's book, we talk as openly and honestly as we can Marvin thought we were honest Doctor indicates that they will probably keep PO. Doctor sees PO alone and tells us that PO is very unhappy. We wait and wait. PO will be given some tests and sent up to a ward. We smoke [cigarettes], PO presents us with problems, the car, the farm, the typewriter for mommy. We promise to take care of them. Finally we go home PO tells us to sleep over. Make phone calls from here I take JL to my house to sleep over. Next day ---

Next day here, on Friday we found out what ward PO was on and tried to find out his doctor, we called Dr. Carl Reinzler and Dr. Ed Podvell and Bernie Weitzman and got some opinions etc. We were wondering whether to leave PO in Bellevue or not. Later Dr. Elfenbein (PO's doctor at Bellevue) called and told us that PO was on the best ward, in fact the ward that the admitting doctor had recommended. She knew who PO was and had attended poetry readings by AG & PO and in fact had been on some kind of Buddhist retreats herself. I liked her over the phone. JL and I went up to see PO. He was ashen colored and puffy and very withdrawn, and silent walking eyes closed and bumping into things. JL drew him out somewhat and got PO to smile a bit. Po did express strong wish to leave. I was impressed that ward looked ok – I had seen much worse in old days working at Chicago State Mental Hospital -- no one nodding out in chairs or restrained. We talked to doctor Elfenbein that day and gave her a copy of <u>Clean Asshole Poems</u>. We saw PO on Sat. and he was still bad looking but slightly more with it still wanting to get out quick and not too clear on how or why he had got there. Monday PO looked much

Joe Gross is an old doctor friend. I get the feeling he is a Dr. Feelgood. Eugene is Allen's brother, the lawyer.

better, over worst of de-tox, and conversing normal, eyes open. Everyday PO has gotten clearer and clearer about his problems. Right now he even suggesting a short in hospital stay at VA alcohol abuse to ease transition home, he told JL that he is digging the ward, looking at other crazies and seeing himself or not seeing himself and thinking about himself and building his courage. Recovered alky members of sangha have been visiting and advising and will take PO to various AA groups. PO is still set on giving Cherry Valley to Buddhists a thought I don't relish and Eugene certainly has no love for but if it must be it must be anyways it's on hold. A fellow (Dan Nelson) is now staying at the farm. Now Allen, from what I can see and what I have learned – you are in classic role of THE ENABLER it is a role that must stop not only must you not give PO money to drink (establish trust fund?) but you will have to examine your part of the total equation I.E. how do you get your hook out of PO? I know this is complicated but it seems subtly that you are hedging your bets against JL and hoping to keep dependent PO to serve for you longer. PO is going through big period of denial of his feelings for you and this too will have to be aired. All in all real therapy for all concerned is probably called for. This whole case may shake up the sangha who all too freely say "crazy wisdom" in reference to someone suffering mental anguish (that's not my observation but a sangha member's) Why was PO never given therapy? Further subjugation to stronger will? You are a key player here and I sincerely hope that you check in with JL, myself, or a physician we set up to ensure that no slightly barbed comments cause giant backsliding. I am also reminding JL that if you rec'd some attention from PO, you wouldn't feel compelled to "bug" them. . . Of course the whole scene is ingrown with JL working for you and PO living off you. PO needs to make some of his own money. Sangha member (recovered alky) has light moving business maybe source of work. Today we learned that PO's liver might be in very bad state. More details when they are known. I hope you don't resent me talking personally about your major love. I feel that I have taken charge for a little while and though I wish to back out at the right time I still feel responsible for PO and think that a true threshing out of the problems can only benefit all involved. I gotta finish up here. I hope you realize that I bear strong love for both you and PO and that these thoughts are my own.

Now Shelley's blouse size is medium or 36. Juanita wants a robe like a morning robe bright pretty color please (red?) I will send business news and copies of things soon. I hope your bronchitis is easing.

    Much love

      Bob

———

These events void my emotions. I stop at the plywood desk to collect my sanity; write this letter as tight as possible. Now I only recall the contents of the letter but I have no memory of writing it. I liken it to labor pains forgotten by new mothers.

Allen and I have a few brief phone conversations between China and New York. My letter takes a while to reach him. He sends this reply after digesting my letter. I am too dazed to feel very proud of my own actions. However I treasure Allen calling my work *heroic*. I am aware that I have acted like a father should for a child who is in distress.

Your handling of Peter's crisis seems heroic. Except for the awful stress on you it may be better that I wasn't there. I might have panicked or been too Cool & avoided Bellevue Confrontation which may be a good think thing. Though it seems you bear the weight of my own family troubles which is unfair . . .

Your handling of peter's Crisis seems heroic. Except for awful stress on you it maybe better I wasn't there I might have panicked or been too Cool + averted Bellevue Confrontation which may be a good think thing. Tho it seems you bear the weight of my own family troubles which is unfair.

In my earliest years with Allen, I am the father figure. Putting order and borders to objects and people seems natural to me while I myself experience real fatherhood for the first time. I still strongly believe that it is not an accident that Peter breaks down when Allen goes away and leaves me to manage. He attacks me because he knows that I will set limits and more importantly he knows that I will enforce them. He needs to detoxify and to start therapy but the ugly first step is for me to call the police.

The rooms on 12th Street seem empty and quiet. The sun still drenches the church steps. The pigeons still line up under the cornice. I use the newfound peace to collect myself. Walking to the post office again is comforting. Waiting in line is a luxury. I am immersed in ruminations about what I really think I am doing in Ginsberg's world.

Meanwhile 1984 is a huge year for Allen as my semi-comic press release shows.

ALLEN GINSBERG
P. O. BOX 582
STUYVESANT STATION
NEW YORK, N. Y. 10009

TEN TOES IN THE ORIENT

Naropa's own, Allen Ginsberg, has been invited to the Peoples Republic of China by the Beijing Writers' Association. Gary Snyder is also a part of the American delegation. The writers will attend the Beijing Writers' Association meetings and then sightsee for several weeks. After the other writers return to write their articles for the New Yorker, etc. Allen will stay on to teach two weeks each at two major universities Hebei U. in Baoding and Fudan U. in Shanghai. Allen has assembled a small library of his favorite American poets to donate to the universities and will be teaching American poetry (Crane to Antler). Meanwhile his life work--Collected Poems 1947-1980-- is being beautifully printed and bound under red and gold Harry Smith covers by Harper & Row, publication date Jan. 2, 1985. This coming January will also mark a showing of Allen Ginsberg's photography over the last three decades at Holly Solomon Gallery in New York City. Many photographs have been printed for the first time ever. Also look for a giant Ginsberg/Burroughs spread in Vanity Fair, new poems in the American Poetry Review, and major articles on Allen in The New York Times magazine and the Atlantic Monthly. This may mean Allen has done everything he ever hoped to except appear nude in the New York Times...By the by, we have it on good word from Mr. Peter Orlovsky that we may expect Allen to return home fully equipt with a Tibetan Bride and baby boy.

Congratulations!

Bob Rosenthal
the Home Office

I feel I have earned the right to truly understand Allen and I feel I have earned the right to truly understand Allen and Peter's relationship. I have become baffled. Allen tells me that his relationship with Peter is really only good for a year or a year and a half. He understands the dysfunction and the control through money that he exercises over Peter. He can't help himself. I realize that Allen like everyone one else is entitled to dysfunctional love. He flies to Hazleton in Minnesota for a weekend co-dependency workshop. Upon his return he is enthused and energized with a brand new vocabulary to describe his love. Allen agrees that he is the enabler but I don't think he fully swallows it. The 1980s is a decade of getting "on the wagon." There are many twelve-step programs. Narcotics users. Over-eaters. Drinkers. Gamblers. Credit card spenders. Allen feels connected. Peter goes to his therapy sessions. In several months Peter is back on 12th Street. Again the office is being distracted by the inner workings of Allen and Peter and Juanita. I start to think about moving the office out of the apartment. (This doesn't happen until 1988.)

Shelley and I are closing in on our teen years of a monogamous relationship. Allen and I argue about monogamy versus having many sexual partners. Naturally I propose that sexual adventures innovations and growth can all happen between monogamous partners. Allen feels that growth only comes through a growth in numbers of partners. His idea must endure a particularly pernicious malevolency. Jealousy!

Allen's poetry business is growing. There are more poetry readings. Publication requests. Interviews. Meetings. Conferences. Piles of writings to proof. The phone rings with greater frequency and urgency. People need advice on *how to* start a poetry magazine or a reading series. They ask where does a student find the funds necessary to bring Allen to their school?

———
Peter is only sexually servicing Allen. If this bothers Allen, he can still believe his own mythology.

———
Marriage means monogamy in 1984. The gay community is not broadly advocating legal marriage yet.

———
Shelley and I know several couples practicing *open* marriages. Each one ends in divorce.

———
Go to student activities; they have the big bucks for rock bands!

People are often in distress or in need of solace. I send them a Buddhist Eightfold Path handout. It offers a straightforward approach to righting one's ways. Gregory sees a copy of this gospel on the desk. As a joke he grabs it. Starts to read it out loud changing the words. I am laughing so hard I grab my sides. Gregory takes a thick pencil and marks up the whole document. He turns the simple rules into poetry. Gregory's version seems designed to be somewhat more disquieting than the reassuring aid I usually send out.

Understanding The Four

life
    comes from desire
achieved by walking
be always firm in your
    intent to walk
be friendly
    don't show disrespect
Try to do everything
    as well
    living decently
keep up the path
the situation you are in
may properly
    respond to that situation
learn teaching
    by learning how

THE EIGHTFOLD PATH

1. RIGHT KNOWLEDGE. Understanding the four ~~truths~~. ~~Life is suffering that~~ ~~suffering~~ comes from desire; ~~that desire can be broken; breaking desire is~~ achieved by walking ~~the eightfold path~~.

2. RIGHT INTENTION. Be always firm in your intent to walk ~~the eightfold path~~.

3. RIGHT SPEECH. Be friendly ~~do not insult, speak ill, use coarse or~~ ~~with words~~. *don't show disrespect*

4. RIGHT ACTION. Try to do everything as well ~~as possible~~.

5. RIGHT LIVELIHOOD. ~~Earn your~~ living decently.

6. RIGHT EFFORT. Keep up the ~~energy needed to continue on the~~ path.

7. RIGHT AWARENESS. ~~Know~~ the situation you are in, ~~so you~~ may properly respond to that situation.

8. RIGHT MEDITATION. Learn ~~what the intellect cannot~~ teach, by learning how to ~~banish thoughts from your mind~~. *ING* ^

IS/ACTS: A Meditation on the Middle Way

The student desiring ~~the results of~~ true discipline must cultivate the attitude of unceasing ~~clear alertness~~. And what is this alertness? It is the ~~seeing of all~~ ~~things in their true~~ fashion. And again, what is the nature of this true seeing? It is not seeing things as matter, or as shape; it is not seeing things as eternal, or as changing. 'Eternal' is one end; 'changing' is another. Everything IS, is one end. Everything ACTS, is another end. The middle between the extremes of IS and ACTS, this cannot be touched, compared, seen, known, or found. This is the Middle Way. Living in the center of this IS/ACTS, without thought for being or for action, this is the result of true discipline.

from the Ratnakutha Sutra
translated by William J. Higginson

for Bob Rosenthal
from Gregory

Business shake up. I lobby Allen to take over Charlie's job. Allen agrees. I start to agent Allen's performances for a 10% cut. Charlie is gracious about it and probably sees it coming before I do.

I am well connected at Allen's desk. I am facilitating the connectivity of Allen's universe. Routinely, I am allowed to dialogue with my heroes.

I adore the poetry of flowers and fields. Love the thread of vitality that binds painterly images and urban sensibilities. James Schuyler lives in the home of Fairfield and Ann Porter in the Hamptons before moving into the Hotel Chelsea. Ann Porter supports James Schuyler through the Committee on Poetry. Every month we receive a maintenance check for Jimmy. Each month I fail to mail Jimmy his check at the Chelsea until he calls me. Soon it is just a fun ritual. Jimmy is one of my poetic heroes. His talk embraces the way rice pudding tastes. It becomes heavenly to me. We gossip about "bad" Tom and "good" Helena. I note Jimmy's deeper commitment to the Anglican Church. Allen respects Jimmy as a poet but I don't think he looks to Jimmy as a model. Allen likes to connect dots in people's minds more than he likes to paint an entire picture.

1982. Allen lets Simon Pettet and me use Committee on Poetry Inc. to raise funds to host a festival of British Poets in downtown New York. Eric Mottram poet and American Poetry scholar in England makes a rare appearance. Guinness Beer Co. contributes cash and kegs.

October. Allen Inc. pays Ted Berrigan to walk off with several brown shopping bags of **Junk Mail**. We have done this before and since. Ted's job is to first sort the letters. Check for mistaken inclusions of **Literary mail**. Then utilize the **Junk Mail** as the basis of an original poem. Ted works on the poem and often talks to me about it. It is tantalizing as he describes the process of finding the lines. Condensing them into a **Junk Mail** sonnet. The more he works on it the less ready it seems. Finally he claims it is ready. It is indeed a sonnet. Sits in his journal. He dies before we ever get to see or hear the poem. The journal is not found.

1983. We receive a letter from Bill Morgan. He is working

How many poetry universes pay poets to write an assigned poem?

This is our last check to Ted. When I get the call about Ted, I am in my parents' house. My father is struggling with dementia and I am feeling as alone as I did as a child. Ted teaches me volumes in the tightness of his upper lip. Silently, he believes in me and verbally quavers "Oh, you fucking Jews!"

on an annotated bibliography of Lawrence Ferlinghetti. Wants access to the Ginsberg deposit at Columbia. While working there he notices the terrible mess it is in. He also notices that Allen has saved *everything.* It is his idea to compile the first annotated bibliography of Allen.

Bill lives around the corner on Avenue A. Shares the same back courtyard as Allen's apartment. As he works on his bibliography Bill methodically reorganizes Allen's office and archives. Bill teaches us the value of simplicity in cataloging. He is not a fan of Miles' tape index system.

1984. Raymond Foye needs a job. We pay him to catalog the photo collection of Allen's at Columbia. Up until this point the boxes contain a loose series of envelopes without an index. Previous photo researchers may have pocketed original prints. No one would have any way of knowing. Raymond does make lists. He realizes that Allen could have a show of his images. Raymond prints some of the images from the negatives. Shows them to Allen. This sparks Allen's resurgence into the world of photography.

Raymond's new catalog becomes useless in no time because the images are not marked in a way to maintain the order. They are once again hopelessly mixed up. Bill Morgan organizes them and makes it stick.

1984. Allen sends $500 to the Paterson New Jersey Library to buy poetry books. Allen gives money to the Writers Voice to bring Philip Whalen for a New York reading. Allen pays Harry Smith to render Allen's sketch drawn in India of *Buddha's Footprint* three fish design. Harry creates an effective logo for all Allen Inc.'s

————

Bill is tall and fully framed. His hair is short in a 1950s butch haircut. His genial manner easily fits in at the office as the typical straight guy.

————

Raymond arranges and curates Allen's first show of photography at the Holly Solomon Gallery.

commercial use. Harper/Collins book spines. Bank checks. Stationary. Don Cherry performs with Allen at Folk City on June 15th. During a performance of "Hūm Bom" Cherry sings out on stage. "We don't wanna bomb." Allen is surprised and pleased. Takes up the phrase and creates new verses for the evolving song.

———

The day Ted dies is almost funny. It is the date we falsely print on our mimeo mag *Caveman:* July 4th, 1983.

He writes some memorable lines for that issue. Lorna Smedman is mad about it for years. Ted writes, "How could someone so round be so square?" Lorna is steamed up but after I puke a little in her lap in the car coming home from Murat's party, she forgives me completely. This proves how little I comprehend anger.

———

We are successful in bringing poets from Europe, China, India, Japan, and the Caribbean to the city and in finding prestigious venues for them like the Brooklyn Museum, Museum of Modern Art, the Great Hall of the Cooper Union, and the Band shell in Central Park, U.C.L.A., Woodland Pattern, Milwaukee, Santa Fe, NM.

Ted's death on July 4 1983 changes the balance of the Lower East Side poetry continuum. Poets start to drift off. Move into nicer apartments. Marry. Find "real" jobs. My boys are taking up much of my personal time. Our bookshelves are squeezed so tight with volumes of poetry that one cannot pull any volume out. The stereo is moved to a high shelf that even Shelley can't reach. I am working with poetry comrades to create International Poetry Festivals even though I make no money from it. Shelley chides me for not pouring my organizing skills into the benefit of my entire family. I listen and we begin to seek out urban homesteading opportunities in the Lower East Side.

Anger: Open Your Eyes!

I notice that I am writing fewer poems but the poems are getting better. I know that I will not be the youngest anything. I admire Yeats for writing great works at the end of his life. The urge to write poems remains. In fact becomes stronger. A poem forms like an aura around me until I stop long enough in front of a piece of paper. Several of our friends die in sudden ways. I begin to use a Frank O'Hara model. Writing an acrostic poem for a deceased friend using their name as first letters to lines. Titling the work *Poem*. Soon I have a dozen of these poems.

Peter Orlovsky is still breaking down and at times doing damage that Allen pays for. Busting Peter with police ride to VA psych is getting easier. Allen learns to do it himself. Peter is more compliant and sits still for cuffing. The police get to know Peter and the rides back go smoothly.

In February, 1985, Peter trashes the super's apartment in the basement by smashing furniture and guitar amps – racking up damage of $500. Another $500 worth of damage in the same apartment occurs in March.

Peter begins a wicked cycle that lasts many years. When Peter's government check comes he holes up in his apartment. Binges on anything he can. Alcohol. Crystal meth. Cocaine. Crack.

Allen wins. Only Peter is losing. I don't care. I am turned to stone.

Pills. When the funds are exhausted he goes into deep remorse curled up into a fetal position. He gets up when the next check arrives. The junkie's shame and guilt is even harder to endure than the pathos of a drug addict's addiction. The drug is a flying spirit. The come down is a pit of selfish quicksand. Juanita hangs in until the end of 1986. Surprisingly through the slough of his drug behaviors Peter keeps another girlfriend in the picture all the time. This is too much for Juanita. She wisely petitions Allen to help her find a new job. He does. Allen starts to see a psychiatrist as mentioned in *Personals Ad.*

Allen tries to protect me from Peter and to take me out of the financial arrangements with Peter. Peter tries to use me to get money. Allen gives me a note to show Peter if Peter will not let me do my work.

Dear Peter:

Please don't use mental force on Bob Rosenthal to make him break my instructions. Phone me if you have a hassle.

XXXLove

Allen

[The stamp in the lower right corner is Allen's seal with his Buddhist name: Lion of Dharma.]

This period in my service to Allen seems clouded. My head is bowed by the psychic weight of hating Peter. The slow burn is different from the hot flash of anger. One is not aware of anger until the heat is searing.

In the office, Harry and I snidely nickname him Dorian when Allen is not around.

The difficult year makes me bold enough to address many of my ongoing concerns. An annoying one is the way Allen capriciously runs the office (hiring his young lovers). I observe that I am being treated like a square lug to be ignored. I feel that Allen no longer appreciates me. My friends tell me that I have worked for Allen long enough. More is not good for me. I am too deeply immersed in Allen's affairs. I can only think to try to improve my lot by bettering my position in the office.

Raymond Foye confuses me. I really like him but am convinced that he does not like me. He forgets to invite Juanita and me to the party after Allen's Holly Solomon photo-show opening. Allen carries an old torch for Raymond who looks perfectly angelic. Seems eternally youthful. I send off a third person list of all my complaints to Allen. The Irwin persona most likely helps me to detach mere grumblings from my more reasoned complaints.

1. BR salary, $10,000./year plus commissions on reading, photo?

2. Office expenses including salaries should come out of doing business i.e. user fees for people using office materials or staff example: Miles, Aronson, Peter? Fees to myself under this arrangement would be addition to salary.

3. AG must treat old friends with whom he has professional relations in a Pro manner. i.e. complete sloppiness Raymond Foye arrangements including uncertainty as to future of negs, commissions, (negs must be in a vault under AG name.) Ray maintains completely Pro relation to AG. Wanted job when broke and got it, pleaded with BR for higher hour wage and got it ($7/hr) but abandoned Columbia work to move into more lucrative areas of Museum sales and gallery showings/sales. Ray takes Pro 20% while at least in part being paid to organize shows and museum sales. BR will not accept RF making more $ [than himself]off AG in given year. Or Charlie [Rothschild] – he charged AG Pro rates but is rude and slovenly to AG and AG staff.

4. BR wants $1,000. bonus [commission never received from PO NEA Fellowship] as per promise of AG.

5. AG must not agree to do readings without coordination with BR. BR gets messages like, "AG told me to tell you it was OK." (low pay readings) OK to do peanut readings but no surprises please.

6. Office needs new typewriter, pref. a great electronic one etc.

7. Need to install built in lock on office door.

8. BR recommends that Cherry Valley be neither donated nor sold.

9. Restricted access from Peter.

10. Allen, don't be smug about giving it all away. Be mindful of old age, extended staff, and heirs.

11. On the subject of being mindful: please realize the extent to which AG dumps (or abandons to) AG neglects, fuck-ups, changes onto BR. Upshot if BR accepts responsibilities must also be accorded courtesy of involvement in major decisions.

Allen equivocates about Raymond but agrees to sort out these issues. I am jealous of Raymond. The money worries are a subterfuge. Most of the confusion is caused by Allen's cock-driven way of doing too many things.

———

No lock on office door and no Peter O. commission.

———

Allen's young Chinese friend, Ai Wei Wei, helps us put together a reading tour of poets from China. It is election day when Wei Wei and I take a cab to JFK. I try to explain the Electoral College to Wei Wei and I notice the Sikh driver leaning back to also understand. After we get to the LA motel room, we learn that Reagan is elected. Wei Wei comes out of the shower in a towel and berates me and America. "At least Mao is a good poet!"

———

Johnny Stanton and I write a play about the Ted Berrigan household on St. Mark's Place. Steve Carey and I start to write a play about the rediscovery of the Erie Canal until Gary Lenhart informs us that the canal is still there. "You can see it from the thruway!"

I actually get most of my demands. Become closer to being treated as a full partner. The income is always a slight yet persistent factor for me.

End of the 1980s. I am phasing out of my fatherly "get your act together" persona. I start to be guided by both my real mentor Irwin and elder friend Allen.

Our revenue stream grows ever larger. The bank accounts always hover around zero. I am exacting a higher percentage for Allen's poetry readings. I learn how to negotiate fees up. Now I am working with the world directly as it accesses Allen. I know the editors and the publicists. I know the journalists and the archivists. Far from being an idiot I am a synthesizer of the Ginsberg world before it reaches Allen. If they want to interview Allen I make sure their questions are strong. Suggest further readings if they aren't. I demand extra tapes and batteries. And warn the interviewers to be prepared for Allen's displeasure and utter openness.

I am balancing a zany job with a myriad of personal projects. Allen's observational approach to anger and the calm of yoga are working for me. In fact they help me to maintain a detached concern for Peter Orlovsky's welfare. They allow me to set the limits that Peter craves. My income worries become palpable. Allen offers me a higher salary. When I thank him he smiles a lascivious grin. Greedily rubs his ruddy hands together. "Good! I have spun you deeper into my Karmic web!"

7 Drugs: Just Say Maybe

from *Shadow Loss*

there is no honey in my veins
        there is your bed
     over there
        here is your meal
from the shining pot

————

When I meet with high school students to discuss Allen, they often seek intimate information about drugs, "Is he stoned all the time?"

————

Heroin use is a motif in *Howl*. He chews inhalers of Benzedrine to write *Kaddish* in marathon sessions or alone in the universe a heroin fix to dictate a poem upon the death of Frank O'Hara. LSD becomes universally lyrical in *Wales Visitation*. Mescaline looks at Irwin.

Allen's trips are not only his own but they are known through his writings.

————

Being a teenager in the late 1960s exposed me to lots of ditch weed.

Even as I clean New York apartments in the mid-1970s, pot is still prevalent and mild. It is perceived as less pernicious than alcohol and safer than alcohol in terms of the commission of regretful behavior.

I NEVER SEE ALLEN USE ANY DRUG to *get high*. This is exactly what most people do. The intent is to kill time and memory. Allen's intent is to enjoy time by being aware of memory. Marijuana is a nice aperitif before a trip to the Museum of Modern Art to visit a Cézanne. Allen never thinks that creativity comes from a drug. Rather he believes in doing a task. My answer to students' queries regarding Allen's personal drug use is "No. Allen does not use drugs to meditate or watch a movie. Ginsberg uses drugs to accomplish a task. Allen is a workaholic. Not a drug addict. He is not even a habituated user." Sometimes the truth disappoints. Allen has a curiosity about drugs. He dabbles in their use. Always keeps shy of habits that hinder his work.

Allen is an avid propagandist for the decriminalization of the addictive opiates and speed. He endorses an enlightened attitude towards social drugs such as marijuana and LSD. His concerns are focused towards getting his strung-out friends into treatment on demand. He keeps a small stash of pot available for young men who accompany him home after a late mushroom barley soup at the Kiev. I bet that he smokes with them for their ease. Pot is not coercive. Discussing possible sex is one of Allen's objectives. In a group photograph Allen grabs the joint. Appears to be passing it to his neighbor. Late in his life he tells a reporter from the *New York Times* that he smokes pot several times a week. I confront him. "What happened to candor? You don't smoke pot that much!"

"How do you know?" he retorts peevishly.

I think but don't say. "I outta know! I'm a pot head."

Allen places high spiritual value on LSD. Marijuana is only a pleasant hobby. Pot. Weed. Grass. Joints. Smoke. Allen likes the 40s jazz word *muggles*. Weed grows everywhere. Its intoxication is less intense before freaks take over its botany. Pot becomes socially acceptable in small stages. A movie reference. A comedy routine. Allen passing the joint while smiling to camera. Grass is an underground culture that is emerging as acceptable. Allen Ginsberg is pleased but not excited. Allen says that pot is a reality kick!

1943. Teenage Allen meets William Burroughs. The older William tutors Allen in shooting heroin. Allen's introduction to drug use is purely social. Luckily he does not become addicted. Allen keeps his old set of "works." A venerable glass hypodermic syringe. Attachable metal needles. It lives in a little pharmaceutical box stuffed into a lone beige sock in the drawer. There among faded rolled pairs just in case. I like to look at it. It gives me shivers just to hold it.

Allen's junkie friends grow old. William. Gregory. Herbert. Each is long lived. Allen wants them to receive medical treatment rather than fear of arrest. Allen explains that heroin itself although addictive is not dangerous to life and limb. Dirty needles are a danger. Committing crimes to buy the drug is dangerous. The supply is tainted. William. Gregory. Herbert. All survive hardcore addictions. I puzzle why none of Allen's old junky friends come down with AIDS. I figure it is that the hardcore junky does not share anything. Not works. Not shit!

Allen spends decades collecting raw data on narcotic drug use. This includes the hypocrisy of the United State's government policies. Since the 1960s his newspaper clippings establish that CIA drug deals in Southeast Asia support covert operations in Cambodia. The eight dirty green file drawers are the basis for several articles and at least one book. Researchers come to Allen's filing cabinets to peruse his faded yellow press clippings (FYPC Allen's coinage) to jump-start their research.

LSD is a family connection for Allen. His first experiment with psychedelic drugs is through his cousin Dr. Oscar Janiger. He is a pioneer in LSD experimentation. The original work is done for the US Military. There is hope it could be a real truth serum. Allen has a myriad of psychedelic adventures with Timothy Leary. The Hells Angels. The Human Be Inn. *Wales Visitation*. I am not sure when or if Allen drops acid again. He gives it to poets from the Soviet East like Andrei Voznesenski. Allen comes home with a vile of LSD tablets to put in his freezer. Stanley Owsley (LSD originator) gives it to Allen at a psychedelic conference in California. Allen asks Owsley if it is good. Owsley replies that no one would give him bad stuff. In the vial with the LSD pills is a note to guests. "Do not use without my or Bob Rosenthal's permission. Allen." I give myself permission.

In *Capitol Air*, Allen writes, *If you're feeling confused, the government's in there for sure.*

Government is a drug. It feeds upon us and we pay it with our health and our lives. The illusion of being justly governed is an addiction. Allen avoids such addictions. William tutors him to read between the lines and to write between the lines. Allen is obsessed with his government. He worries about it. He addresses it in public. He collects the truth on government police agencies dealing drugs. Does he understand that in Russia he is dead for being openly gay, and exposing government police hypocrisy? Of course he does. But that can never be the point! In 1965, Allen is persona non grata in Russia and the USA. He never stops thinking about the government.

Alfred McCoy is investigating here for his book *The Politics of Heroin in Southeast Asia*.

Allen asks Andrei, "Where in Russia did you take that acid?" Andrei laughs hard and exclaims, "Are you fucking crazy? I took it immediately in the Chelsea Hotel!"

My earliest experiments are with weird pills in college that have skull-and-crossbones on them. It is rumored that they contain strychnine, a known hallucinogen and toxin. LSD seems to sweep away cobwebs of afterthought, and place the voyager onto an empty plane that is a reedy void.

Emptiness is the best part of the trip and scariest to a fragile emotional constitution. The inner void can be the source of bad trips. Nakedness is a lasting image. It is how we now see ourselves even though we have put our clothes back on.

David Henderson tells me he was at Chappaqua, with Allen in the 1960s when there was a lot of LSD happening. He remembers Allen saying, "You can take LSD and soar angelically and see the solutions to the world's problems but then you must come down." David pauses and widens his eyes. This point of "come down" is where most trippers end their observations but *not* Allen. "Back on the ground, you see that the road to these solutions is paved with a multitude of detailed tasks to be accomplished." Clearly LSD is to see the big road map but is no more than mirage on your actual journey.

Hard-ons wither under a speed regime. For Allen, a prick made flaccid by speed is a modern biblical abomination.

I am on the bed at home sitting cross-legged next to a red cotton Oriental rug covering the flaking plaster wall. Meditating on being nothing but a reedy breath. Colors have a dull intensity that throb in rhythm with my slow respiration. I am a breeze flowing through a piece of bamboo. Allen telephones to discuss business. I inform him that I am tripping. He seems pleased. Advises me to "concentrate on emptiness." "Yes. Sir!"

Importantly Allen is a beautiful and fearless writer on the topic of psychedelics. His essays on LSD are among his finest prose writings. They uplift with a transcendental energy reminiscent of Henry David Thoreau. This is found in his testimony on drugs to congress. His speech *Public Solitude* in the Arlington Church in Boston 1967 is inspiring. He boldly claims that psychedelics allow people to transcend habituated perceptions. Alter people's consciousness going forward. He uses the ritualized sharing of a spiritual drug to bring together those who are held back by their own *fear-traps*. LSD is the catalyst for Allen to diffuse the animosity the Hells Angels have for anti-Vietnam War demonstrators. Reduce the protestors' fear of the motorcycle clubbers. Allen becomes increasingly aware of the prevalence of drug abuse on college campuses. He decides to clarify his message. Any use of a drug (be it pot or peyote) is only for *serious* spiritual exploration.

Allen hates "speed." He sees it destroying Peter Orlovsky and others. The speed family empowers the user with clarity of purpose. It is not a drug associated with spiritual depth. The Beat writers take junk. Speed. Acid. The New York School poets drink. The St Mark's poets pop uppers and downers. The stated rule at the Cherry Valley farm is No Needles.

Gregory Corso. Herbert Huncke. Ray Bremser. Arrive at the East Hill farm to dry out. Secretly shoot up. One cannot separate a junky from his or her needle. Allen makes a rule but never polices his friends. He dotes on their weaknesses. Admires their work no matter the individual cost each artist suffers. Gregory doesn't need hidden drug references in his poetry. He is a classicist. He needs the junk to take him to the place where he stands on the ancient shore of wisdom and clarity. I do not comprehend how much Gregory hates his own sanity. I am walking in Union Square with Gregory. I am taking him to the bank to cash a check. Gregory looks downtrodden. He is on methadone. That drug never satisfies him. "Wouldn't it be great if you just had a clean cheap legal supply of heroin so you could just live your life with less hassle?" I preach. Gregory looks at me sharply "No way. Bobby! I want to kick this junk. I want to be clean!" Gregory is a heavy user. Five bags a day. I am moved by that pure space within him that exists unsullied by decades of abuse.

Painkillers make work possible. The aging Allen keeps a supply of synthetic morphine pills (Demerol) on him at all times to overcome gout or kidney stone pain or exhaustion. He pushes himself professionally. Often uses a painkiller to get up on stage. Allen is larger than life on stage. He shakes his frame and bellows out his poems and songs. After the party he limps home to crash. Slogs to the airport to fly home. Allen uses drugs to finish his poetry reading tours. This is his most private use. His most basic use. Probably most toxic use.

The Demerol allows Allen to work through fatigue. It shortens his days on earth. The rigorous reading schedule is hell on Allen's frame. No drug high compares to performing poetry to

The whiteness of the whale is a pure snow hill of drug. Can Ahab stop? Allen here is the Pequod. He forgives all and always offers love. Allen's commitment to the journey is total. There is no safe harbor when one sails beyond prescribed societal laws.

I have no stories of sharing a silent sunset with Allen, thick pot ash on our beards. However, there are several roach clips lying around. One is Florentine, long and delicate. Another favorite looks like an ordinary door key but it opens to receive the roach. Allen never carries it. Why should he? The entire world is his drug dealer! Allen is not wrong in *America: The whole world is serious but me!* Three decades later, Allen is the only one who is serious.

attentive faces. Hanging on one's every word. The painkiller only forestalls the rest that his exhaustion requires. The sessions of crashing grow deeper and longer. After a reading tour Irwin goes to bed for more than a day. His frailness is revealed under the heavy quilt. It is quietly alarming but his energy returns. He rises yet gimpy. Goes forth to do battle again.

Allen likes to sing his exuberant upbeat song *Dope Fiend Blues*. *I'm naturally a dope fiend under empty skies!* Yes! This blues song has an unrepentant love of using drugs. Allen confesses on stage that he does not really know what the message is. The song is fun to sing. The needle delivers the stuff. The smoke carries the high. The pharmacy dispenses the plastic vials. Allen delivers the poetic tranquility of his poems through needling. Smoke in one's eyes. Bitter pills. An ecstatic sense of victory that is realization. Allen completely spends himself physically in his work. Ironically the work is to ease human suffering.

8 Neighbors Charnel Ground

Relay

long lavender lines
    school kids
        ready to run
relay with a purple cord
portly man blows whistle

all the sun on East 11 Street
suddenly cheers thick boys
    winsome girls
their dark hair flowing after them
    like this night after evening
me after you
I say a dumb thing
    full of snide self
deprecation
intent to harm
to unload vagaries of failure
    onto your broad palms
though we do not forgive the night
kids run hard down the blacktop
is there hope I can
    take back the
baton

drop it beneath your panting feet
like Moses threw down his staff
    which wiggles
away
can the Pharaoh that binds the
people in your blood
let me go
    to you
split the seas of peevishness?

leaves are turning downtown
    the harvest is in
we can leave this block with its
flag flutters
    chocolate breezes
wander lower east side through
    short days
find the corners
    that always say
walk
I will always be reaching this baton
    out to you

Peter Stuyvesant wants a beautiful farm outside the city of New Amsterdam. To the East of his home and chapel (now St Mark's Church) is a long stretch of salt marsh leading to the banks of the East River. Stuyvesant likes to hang lost Quakers up by their feet. He fights the home office in Amsterdam to eliminate Asher Levy and the first Jews in lower Manhattan. How fitting that Stuyvesant's farm should fill in with the America's undesirables and misfits and of course the singers of the sodden streets, poets!

ALLEN MOVES INTO THE LOWER EAST SIDE on East 2nd Street in the summer of 1958. His apartment is cheap. Sunny windows face downtown as he pens evocative lines in *Kaddish: There is a little girl from Russia, eating the first poisonous tomatoes of America, frightened on the dock then struggling in the crowds of Orchard Street – but toward what?* East Village? Downtown? Alphabet City? For Allen it is always the Lower East Side. It is his neighborhood. His safe harbor. His playground. Herbert Huncke takes an apartment in the same building as do more junkies.

This neighborhood is the first Manhattan neighborhood to be built on the early 19th Century grid plan for the city. The Lower East Side streets above Houston are numbered and the avenues are lettered. Tompkins Square sits in the middle of the growing neighborhood.

———

Ginsberg's cartography of LES:
1952 - 206 East 7th Street,
1958 - 170 East 2nd Street,
1964 - 704 East 5th Street,
1965 - 408 East 10th Street,
1975 - 437 East 12th Street,
1996 - 405 East 13th Street.
Allen keeps a continuous home in LES for more than forty-five years.

The rent seems laughably low. The landlords come to the door in their grey overcoats to collect the rent. People work poorly paid jobs. Mind their own business. Bohemians move in for the cheap pads. Nobody cares if they party. Are homosexual. Smoke pot. Hang around in pajamas for weeks on end. The artists have no visible means of support. Sometimes fragrant vapors and conversations leak into the hallways. The door is left ajar. It is a social offense everywhere but east of First Avenue. Yogurt and wheat germ sit exotically on the kitchen sideboard. Mixed race couples don't attract dirty looks. Roosters crow at dawn. Heroin is quietly shot up in dark stairwells. People sleep on the park benches.

Allen comes home after spending many years in India. Long hair. A beard. Harmonium. Beads. Finger cymbals. Incense. Hindu holy hymns to chant (Bhakti Yoga). Mudras to practice while sitting cross-legged. He fits in perfectly. Allen's look has fully blossomed. A ruddy-mirrored string bag dangling at his side. Pens and notebooks safely tucked within.

Allen walks on First Avenue. On most blocks a passerby says "Hi!" Allen bows slightly. Looks deeply into their eyes. Returns the greeting. Beggars are always happy to see him coming down the sidewalk. The workers at the Mee Noodle shop (13th Street & 1st Avenue) know him as "No Salt." At four in the morning Allen strolls to the Kiev at 7th and 2nd Avenue for mushroom barley soup. Then on to the Gem Spa at St. Mark's Place to pick up the *New York Times*. He sits up in his bed in his white underwear to consume the *Times* from cover to cover. The Lower East Side is his home. It is where he is from. **He knows his neighbors. Observes the changing story of the streets in his poems.**

I pick up my kids from the Asher Levy School on East 11th Street. We stroll up 1st Avenue to the Palermo Bakery. Buy lemon cookies for now. Semolina bread for dinner. I have crayons and game books back at the office. I manage to work a little longer. Then we head home. Eventually Allen buys a television. It distracts them longer.

I teach a children's writing workshop at the Poetry Project at St. Mark's Church. My young students and I explore the neighborhood with a map of Stuyvesant's farm with the modern grid superimposed. I am publishing poems in small magazines and organizing Poet's Theater nights. In the Lower East Side I am an artist. Parent. Neighbor. Allen is a blessing and a benefactor. No one confuses me with Allen.

My family spends the summer of 1980 in Boulder. I work for Allen and Naropa. Here I am viewed as only Allen's secretary. At a crowded party I hear someone call me "New York Jew."

Allen is often being offered extravagant vacations. He has been offered mountain escapes in Hawaii. Sojourns to the hanging gardens in Turkey. Spa breaks in Italy. Allen doesn't go on vacation just for relaxation. He goes to visit the close friends that live there. For down time and freedom from public scrutiny he stays home in the Lower East Side.

1988. *Charnel Ground* takes the reader on a neighborhood walk. Allen uses exacting details in a Whitmanesque catalog. He tells tales of neighbors. Friends' sufferings and woes. I am familiar with every image in *Charnel Ground*. I follow Allen's walk down the stairs at the 12th Street tenement. Add details for the stories within. I know the drunk on Avenue A. The depressed workers at the post office. Here I am retracing my steps. The darkened

Near the corner of East 12th street and First Avenue, there are two Italian Mafia storefront social clubs. The old men's club is on the south side and the younger men's club is on the north side. The younger men's club is more active. On one occasion, a dead body lies in the street all day in front of their place. One of their own gone wrong. He is given a bullet to his head as he stands at the phone booth. His corpse lies on the sidewalk, head at the curb, bleeding into a pool in the gutter. Since he is dead, there is no rush for the city to pick him up and he is there all afternoon. When bringing Isaac after school he sees the body through the onlookers' legs. On this day of the month, a crushed pack of cigarettes spilt onto the sidewalk and a bottle of dark beer half poured out is left at the curb where the once lover lay. This little shrine appears monthly for over a year.

———

The point is that in the Lower East Side, one is not a New York anything. People are seen clearly delineated by actual presence.

bus garage now crack den whispers its strange invitations. Enter its world of pain and suffering. While typing up Allen's poem I become Emerson's transparent eyeball that sees all. I am completely immersed by Allen's poem of the neighborhood. I sit in it and read it. I hear the footsteps. See the colors.

Melville sails many years before he can sit home and feel the deck moving beneath his bare feet as he pens *The Whale*. The difference between Jacob Riis's photographs of depravity in the Five Points and Allen's recreating a living vibrant universe in the artifacts of poverty is that poetry is the breathing inner nature of all these images. The Lower East Side lives in simultaneous evocations. LES is Allen's entire world in microcosm just as the oceans are Melville's.

AG Photo of his own block, 1988. Bus terminal is razed.

Allen ventures out any time a police action is near. He witnesses the '88 Police Riot in Tompkins Square. Several years later he counsels the Anarchists at a Tompkins Square Anarchist Rally on proper modes of address. Allen tells them not to chant "Kill Yuppie Scum!" They listen politely. "Thank you, Allen Ginsberg! Kill Yuppie Scum!" He visits the East 13th Street squats before the police tanks come to empty them. The squatters give Allen a tour of the squat.

The Italian Social Club down Allen's block needs to appear less conspicuous. The social club's deep storefront is partitioned. Creates a little business space for the sidewalk trade. The social club is still in the large back room. The first front business is a

"Am I Yuppie Scum because I put on a coat and tie to teach?"

If you use angry words that box the opponent into a corner; it will create a reciprocating air of violence.

Almost all of the squats in the Lower East Side eventually become legal buildings. The 13th Street squats house the Tompkins Square "anarchists" and a legal remedy is not achieved. Allen does not really know the history. He is more the ambassador of the Lower East Side than its historian.

bootblack. A middle-aged black man sits in his shoeshine stand. No customers. After weeks of walking by Allen goes in to have his shoes shined. Allen asks the man why he set up his business here? "There are just poor people here!"

"Oh no sir. It's the poor people that are my best customers!"

Allen tells the office about this. We all laugh ourselves silly except for Allen. Everyone knows it is a mafia front. So does Allen. But only Allen cares about the lonely bootblack in the window.

1970s and 1980s. The Lower East Side is a human garden. First Avenue is littered with butchers bakeries green grocers. Cucumbers are here. Oranges are there. East 7th Street has the Thursday store that only opens once a week to sell Jersey farm eggs and apple cider. There is a new-shoes-from-the-fifties store where Shelley fulfills Imelda Marcos' dreams of owning dozens of pairs of practical shoes. We wait in line at Pete's Spice for the clerk to fill our bag with wheat berries. My writing window is perched on the sixth floor above East 11th Street. I watch the Empire State Building sparkle with flash photography as the evening darkens. I imagine the faces in those pictures smiling with the Lower East Side as their background. I watch the children play in Asher Levy schoolyard. I write my poems about the chocolate breezes drifting up the block from Veniero's Pasticceria.

Allen's offices on 12th Street are still busy with Peter's recovery and new breakdowns. I decide that Allen might be able to concentrate better on his work if we move the office to a new location. We find an office two blocks away at 2nd Avenue and 14th Street. We share office space with Alene Lee's daughter's proofreading business. William Burroughs is one of Allen's favorite photographic subjects. Allen shoots him with Alene

Allen is an old Lower East Side acquaintance of Ed Koch's. When Koch is mayor, they find themselves together at a small outdoor venue. Allen asks Ed, "What is the latest book of belles-lettres you have read?" Ed replies, "Oh Allen, you really know how to hurt a guy!"

Alene is Kerouac's Mardou Fox in *The Subterraneans*. The real events occur in Paradise Alley, a large building with a courtyard at East 11th Street and Avenue A. The building is run down and the courtyard is frequented by junkies who shoot up, thus the alluring name.

The office is near the top of the Hartford building that is built for artists. Members of the Ash Can school of painters including John Sloan have had studios here.

Lee on the 7th Street roof in the early 1950s. William is tenderly holding Alene's hand. I am always moved by the hetero-sweetness of this image.

We see a lot of Alene during our year on 14th Street. She tells us of her love for Lucien Carr. She fusses over Allen whenever he shows up. The office is oddly laid out. There are three small rooms and a shared bathroom with the proofreading business. Two of the rooms are closely connected and the third office is located down the hall. It is a relief to get away from the daily affairs in Allen's home. Allen focuses better in the new office. He likes having his own space. He often works by himself late into the night.

A year later we lose the 2nd Avenue space. I find a space at 17 Union Square. Allen is proud. "This is a fantasy come true! To have an office in Union Square!" Once again Allen likes working late into the night surveying the lights across Union Square. His desk is set up for him with pencils sharpened. A bottle of glue close at hand. He tells me that having an office in Union Square makes him feel like an adult.

1994. Allen is still living in the three-flight walk-up on East 12th Street. His congestive heart failure makes him short of breath on the stairs. We help carry his bags. Allen tells fascinating stories about Jack Kerouac to cover up his own breathlessness. He stops on a step to deliver the punch line of the anecdote. Of course his helper is all ears. Not aware that Allen is allowing his breath to regain regularity. On the first floor Simon Pettet is on call to help Allen. He lugs Allen's bags and harmonium up

In this picture, by Brian Graham, I am filling the doorway to the hall and Walt Whitman is posted on the closet door; one can see that Allen is just starting to become frail. I am looking strong as a bulwark against Allen's decline to come. Allen has taken his courage from Whitman and he has passed it on to me. But I see nothing here (my eyes are blanks) and I know less than nothing. I do not understand how frail Allen is becoming. I shade myself from my own fear of a future without Allen. I have to be strong and being strong means not being afraid of the future no matter how uncertain it is. When Whitman is old and frail, his friends take care of him in the house in Camden. A group of devoted lovers ease Walt's passage through the last great uncertainty. We will do the same for Allen to ease his stepping off. As soon as this picture is snapped, I turn and call the elevator and we descend into Union Square.

the stairs at odd hours when Allen comes home from the airport. Selling his archives is the only way to afford Allen a living space with an elevator. Allen searches the *New York Times* for a new home in the Lower East Side.

9 Allen, Inc. Friends & Family

HEAVY

I am thinking I carry the beatings I got as a child. I carry them on me – they are the weight I carry on me. Father beat me for not eating fast enough. I was humiliated with food. I was skinny. I, a finicky eater, slim. I hated fat. I hated peas. I hated things. Peas! I hated peas. I hated peas out of a can. I hated mushy peas not as green as in England. He put two peas on my plate and two eyes on me! He would wait. Watch me eat those poison pills of peas. Those vomit-producing unctuous orbs. Watch. Watch. There was no escape. And the big eye was on me. And I couldn't do it. I would take a pea and put it in my mouth – my stomach would tighten – my throat would close – reverse its flow, I'd start heaving ahmm uhmm uho out my nose. I couldn't get it down – jam it on the roof of my mouth (later scrape into toilet bowl) and pretend to swallow. Not daring to meet his glare.

I must annihilate the pain through ridicule. I start deliberately. I camp up the pain to entertain in modern painful Buster Keaton manner. Keaton's pathos is Allen's, I bet.

Gregory steals one of Allen's expensive Blake books. He sells it to Andreas Brown at the Gotham Book Mart. Allen goes up to 47th Street and buys it back. Then Allen and Gregory sit around in Allen's kitchen and discuss what a thief Andreas is! Firstly, Andreas knows Allen doesn't sell his books; secondly Gregory is sick with junk and cannot help himself. Allen's friends cannot steal from Allen because Allen never calls it thieving.

As the Duke of Venice advises in *Othello*, *The robbed that smiles, steals something from the thief.* Allen smiles with forgiveness and compassion and steals indulgence back from those who rob him. His candor protects him and thus his weakness is his greatest strength. I am much less inclined in that direction.

ALLEN IS LIVING on East 10th Street between Avenues C and D. He is knocked down. Dragged into an abandoned building by several kids. Robbed of $60. Allen gazes at the boys benignly as they approach. He looks like an easy mark with his professorial distraction. Easy-to-snatch laden book bag. Allen writes *Mugging* about it. The *New York Times Magazine* prints the poem and gives Allen a fee. The striking concept in Allen's poem is that he cries out OM AH HUM as he is being attacked. The boys must have been somewhat perturbed by the strange intonations from the old man. The force of the mantra is to shatter illusions. Allen notes that they take $60 cash and leave $10,000 worth of poetry in his shoulder bag "on the broken floor." Gregory Corso notes in *Columbia U Poesy Reading – 1975*

> …the New York Times paid him [Allen] 400 dollars
> for a poem he wrote about being mugged for 60 dollars
> O blessed fortune! for his life / there is no thief.

Gregory is right and he is wrong. People do steal from Allen. Foremost among the thieves is Gregory himself.

Allen is never a Faust. He banishes the devil from his world. Success for Allen can only be measured in love units. Yet Allen has a knack for making money. He works for his immediate needs. His needs are varied. The Salvation Army for suits. Ties. Shirts. Pants. Underwear. Chickens are needed to make soup. Blue cheese to spread on bread. The *New York Times* to read. Cheap dinners out with boyfriends are necessary. His furniture is second-hand. Or made for him by carpenters who love him. They hardly charge anything. His bank account balance is always funded and always low.

Allen Inc. is a non-profit organization. This becomes a creed that holds Allen to account. Allen makes money in order to *do the work*. Allen uses his cottage industry and his office to ease suffering in the world by distributing clothes and medicine and books and poetry publications. Allen sees his world as family. He creates money out of loyalty to family.

In my first years in Allen Inc. Allen befriends Howard Klein at the Rockefeller Foundation. Allen applies to the foundation for money for Naropa. He raises a few thousand dollars for several years running. This Rockefeller money is held in a discretionary fund. Only requires a letter. A few phone calls. Allen's friends discuss if it is a bad thing to do. They feel the Rockefeller Foundation represents the hydra-headed monster of unbridled capi-

Allen deducts almost everything he spends from his taxes and so holds on to every receipt, which he stuffs into a divided accordion file. Taking taxis all day seems extravagant; however, he does not own a car. After adding up the receipts for the year's taxi fares, I realize that the sum is far less than owning a car. Donald Wilen is Allen's accountant. Don has been doing accounting work at the National Lawyers' League when Allen meets him. Don's secretary tells me the favorite part of her job is opening up all of Allen's squished up receipts and tallying them.

———

and what is the work? To ease the pain of living. Everything else is drunkin dumbshow.

Memories Gardens

Anger erupts among some admirers when Allen allows a photograph of himself in a seated meditation posture to be used in a GAP ad. Allen requires that a disclaimer appear in the corner of the ad, which states that all the revenue is going to scholarships for Naropa Institute. Allen chooses to fund Naropa's inner city Denver Youth Program for the summer rather than maintain his noncommercial stance. Myles Aronowitz takes the picture and Allen wants to help support him and his young family. Furthermore, Allen is seated in front of his Buddhist shrine with a portrait of Trungpa Rinpoche on it. There are grumblings in the Buddhist community about poor taste. Allen is figuring some freckled face kid with large ears and toothy grin trapped in *nowheresville* America discovers a clue in a GAP ad to make a leap in consciousness.

talism. Allen tells me that he feels good about it. He takes money from the devil. Transforms it by putting it to good work. Allen would not knowingly sell his soul for the Rockefeller fix. Yet he does *like* walking the edge of concern.

Allen's persona does not "sell out." Thus he denies Faustian corruption. Instead he makes a Myshkin compact of purity. Consequently many of Allen's admirers will never forgive Allen for taking money at all. He never violates a principal to not accumulate wealth. However Allen does violate his deeply held principle of penury to help save the world.

Allen insists on paying in small and large groups. I want to take Allen out for lunch on his birthday. He wants to pay but I make a big scene. Adamantly insist on paying. He looks guilty and uncomfortable. I might spoil Allen's birthday by treating him. At times even a prophet must be gracious about accepting gifts.

Money flows out as fast as it comes in. The overall budget is growing but not his wealth. Allen loves to read poetry to college kids. He prefers that I prioritize booking readings. He can earn money by writing. Signing his photographic prints. But he needs those readings. I doubt he stresses about money a moment in his adult life. He lives in the moment. Gives so much away that he can never be poor. Not ever.

Allen enjoys hosting friends. Providing for the family of poets around the world. His kitchen is a fertile space. Meals are taken there but so are thousands of photographs. The *New York Times* is piled up in the window. The Formica card table kitchen table squares off. Harry. Steven. Gregory. It attracts strange young men who wander in at 3AM.

The photograph is snapped by Allen at a party in his kitchen. I am standing on the left. Shelley is in the foreground with Aliah looking at Allen and Isaac interrupted with cake. Behind us are Juanita Lieberman, Kazuko Shiraishi, Gary Snyder, Alice Notley, Simon Pettet, Roland Legiardi – Laura, and others. Someone blurry in the little room off the kitchen is talking to Harry who is hiding there. This is how I see Allen's vision of a world where people are all awake, engaged, and fed. Allen makes a humongous pot of soup, serves bread and cheese, and buys a cake. Although Allen does not follow consistent rules of hygiene, somehow no one gets sick. Allen licks spoons and put them back into the jelly jar but his world is safe and death only a mirage. Allen's menageries of germs are safe to eat!

Harry

You're the one who signs the checks!

Harry Smith lives with Allen in the mid-1980s. Impossible to describe. One might know Harry as the ground breaking film animator. As the field recorder of Peyote rituals. As the editor of the *Anthology of American Folk Music*. These recordings school the 1950s emerging group of folksingers from the Weavers to Bob Dylan. Maybe one knows the old curmudgeon living in a dumpy room at the Breslin Hotel surrounded by collections objects. String figures. Barn keys. Easter eggs. The Breslin closes. Harry moves into Allen's dump on East 12th Street. He is small. Thin with white hair. Criminally neglected teeth. He is surly when drunk. I first encounter him at a film showing of Pull My Daisy with Robert Frank present at Millennium Films. A voice heckles the film "Fifties Art! Fifties Art!" I am introduced to that voice after the film. Harry hears my name and exclaims. "Oh you're the one who signs the checks!"

I like having Harry around although he is trying to one's concentration. He starts to record East 12th street. He has a microphone out the open window twenty-four hours a day. Often he plays the tapes he has already recorded. The windows are open so the Lower East Side is both recorded and amplified. The street noise is coming from the streets in real time. Time sifts through sound. If I hear a fire truck I have no idea if it is in the present or from several days back. Harry gets proficient at discerning the urban soundscape. He hears a siren. Harry explains "that's on Sixth Street and Avenue A." Harry's diet is limited to sugar cigarettes beer milk. Allen takes many pictures of Harry. The iconic one is Harry sitting at Allen's square kitchen table pouring milk from one Ball jar into another.

Sunday 3/13/88 4pm

Bob –

Harry will need boxes from storage & he will give his tape machine in to Sony to Fix. He may borrow ours while it's being fixed if he has anything needs recording

Allen

Bob –

~~Hell~~

Harry will need boxes from storage he will give his tape machine in to Sony to Fix. He may borrow ours while it's being fixed if he has anything needs recording

Allen

3 milk
1 Colt 45
1 sucrose
1 Salem `100's

Julius Orlovsky also stays on 12th Street. Sony Corp. gives Allen a small camcorder to keep. In exchange Allen has to make a small movie. Let Sony have a copy. Allen shoots Harry Julius Peter and himself. It is touching sweet sad unvarnished. Peter forces Julius to do chin ups. Harry walks through holding cassette tapes and muttering. Julius cooks a hamburger. He turns on Allen putting his fist to his eye and other hand flat before his head. "What are you doing?" Allen asks. "Cooking a hamburger." "But what are you doing with your hands?""I am doing what you are doing." Allen calls the film *Household Affairs*. Julius is the star of course.

The Committee for International Poetry hosts the Haitian poet Felix Morrisau Leroy. I walk in on Harry and Felix in deep conversion speaking the West African language Twi. Harry collects objects and acquires areas of knowledge. He reads trade magazines for astronomers. Follows the arcane beliefs of Aleister Crowley. He is not much of a bather but does not smell bad either. I come into Allen's kitchen. Harry is deeply absorbed in making a painting. It is dark and highly textured. He looks up at me. Says proudly that he is painting with shit. I know he means it. The painting doesn't stink but I make him dry it out on the fire escape. I am always friendly with Harry but I don't kiss hug or otherwise touch him as I fear he might break. Harry tells me that he likes me because I never try to kiss him. I come in. He is weeping. He has just read Allen's *Kaddish*. He reads Allen for the first time!

———
Steven Taylor plays guitar for Allen for about a year longer than I have been in Allen's employ. Steven is born in Manchester, England, and studies music at Glassboro State College. Allen is pleased by both his boyish charms and his quiet skills. Steven does not feel the need to outplay Allen. He truly accompanies. When he sings with Allen, Steven fills in the gaps in Allen's voice thus making Allen sound fuller voiced. Allen takes Steven with him on his European tours. Steven also stays over on 12th street and does editorial and sundry jobs for us. Steven notates Allen's songs. He becomes a part of the 1980s punk rock group the False Prophets. His experiences with both Allen and the New York rock scene enable him to create a doctorial dissertation on Punk Rock. He soon becomes a member of the Fugs. I realize that Allen's entire office retinue is straight. This reflects Allen's practical side; no time wasted chasing us.

———
Jerry Hasan, an old Ginsberg and Philip Whalen friend from West Coast mid-sixties journeying, borrows $50 from the office. I make him promise to repay it. He leaves and never pays us back. I can't forget about it. Hey, Jerry, send that dough!

Allen does not write to order or on deadline. No matter the dangling fruit. Not even for the utilitarian Danish Book Bags he always uses. He tours the globe with one over his shoulder until his pens are falling through the threadbare pockets. The shoulder strap is frayed to fringe. A sangha member owns a small store called Chocolate Soup near the Whitney Museum. He sells the bags. He offers Allen enough new ones for everyone in the office if Allen can come up with a poem about Danish Book Bags. Allen refuses. Disappointed Steven and I collaborate on a poem. We hope Allen might sign on to it. We try and try but we are bad at it. Allen refuses to own our poem. No new book bags appear. Allen is offered lucrative writing assignments for magazines. An assignment to write always shuts Allen's creativity down. Dollar bills float between him and his journal. He slams the book shut. Picks up the *New York Times*.

I keep trying to retrieve office items but it is like scooping water with a sieve. I have limited success. When my desk is empty of office necessities like scissors and stapler, I go down two floors and knock on the door of number six. Simon Pettet and Rosebud Feliu argue about which one borrows the stapler and tape dispenser. I just bring the desk items back upstairs.

Bob – Can we Cash this for Gregory? Yes, Gregory

Allen gives Gregory money but once in a while Gregory borrows Allen's money through me. I make him promise to repay. Naturally he fails to do so. I take umbrage and let Gregory know about it. I feel responsible. Allen doesn't care about the money, but I cannot let it go. I give Gregory the cold treatment. He gets pissed. I am sitting at my desk and Gregory is indignantly calling to me from the hall. "You're not Poetman! I am Poetman! You are third string!" I don't argue but I stubbornly remain diffident towards Gregory for several years. He never pays Allen back, and eventually I can't resist returning to affection for Gregory.

Colleges book Allen for a reading and a visit to a class for about $3000. The percentage I make on these bookings is becoming important to me, as my sons need more clothes, shoes, and activities. In 1986, Allen is invited to replace John Ashbery at Brooklyn College as a distinguished professor. With that title, he earns another $75,000 a year. The salary is enough to pay for the Ginsberg home office: two or three paid workers and all the attendant office rent and supplies. Allen travels out to Brooklyn College twice a week. The other times he travels to give readings. Allen's whole income might gross about $300,000 per annum but he deducts all but $8,000 as expense.

1987. February 27th Allen picks up a lush political appeal. Sends a small check for $5 to the National Republican Committee. Over the following ten years Allen receives over $50 dollars' worth of thank you letters solicitations and plastic membership cards. They laud Allen as a sustaining member of the Republican Party. We laugh every time another signed appreciative letter from Ronald or Nancy Reagan arrives.

Allen's reading schedule is becoming heavier. The most effective way to moderate the pace is to raise Allen's reading honorium. Even though Allen is a workaholic his taxable income is always smaller than mine. He luxuriates in second-hand clothes and furnishings. He buys a new dish drainer to replace the hideously moldy old one. I jokingly call him a Yuppie.

Allen Inc. comprises several divisions of art-related activities besides writing. Allen cycles through them. Doting on one art form for a while. Then shifts to another. After he moves from one art form to the next I follow up. Make sure the resulting remunerations come in. The results end up in recording releases with

Music – record new songs and create music to his poems. Take old tapes to ZBS studios at Fort Edwards, New York; restore them.

Photography – several months: shoot film; view contact prints; order enlargements; hand-caption them. Study out kitchen window comprises over twelve thousand images; *Life* magazine publishes "Meaning of Life" photograph from kitchen window series.

Art – Time to play around with the art world "power" elite for a rich week of midnight suppers with the boys. He doesn't have to pay the bill. Collaborate for rare editions. Make etchings for art patrons.

modest financial returns. Literary projects include collections of poetry. Journals. Essays. Interviews. These bring advances on contracts. Additionally I pay attention to sangha needs. Financial giving to a sangha is returned in good karma. Allen is good at rotating his endeavors over a year's time. His powers of concentration in the moment are awesome. We in the office multitask moment by moment in a chaotic household where photography music poetry art Buddhist obligations swim after Allen. All need immediate follow up.

Young Hires

Allen asks me to find work in the office for young men who are currently sleeping with him. This rarely works out well for me. I have to train them and supervise them and usually their work is not even useful. I become frustrated and suggest that Allen just pay them for fucking. This never happens.

Bob – We're almost out of money in account for Bankmachine Allen / Tuesday I told Gregory I'd cash a check Clemente $1200 check for him – Allen [Bob note in corner] GC owes AG $557 obtained under false pretenses Bob

I hire a young poet, Lynn McGee. Lynn is very efficient. She is an Air Force brat; her dad had been the pilot for Vice President Agnew's jet (Air Force Two). She remembers the black box phone in the living room. Lynn works for half a year.

————

I don't touch them. (Thank you, Ted!) Lust is so real that it must be honored. Honor lust by observing it with a kind eye. If a young lady's shirt is revealing, it is not a good idea to stare, giggle, or drool. It is only an accident and there is more important work to do. The sharing of sexual beauty is generous when done in an atmosphere of trust. My status as a married man deems me safe to be around. That might sound incongruous in the sexually permissive office. Yet my role is to remind one and all what straight means. Memory of a breast's curve or shapely bare thigh can become a wonderful collection of accidental moments. Stolen kisses are the sweetest. Unpiloted lusts are cherubic paintings in the Sistine Chapel of the cranium.

————

Allen's "friends" pressure him for signed photographs. Allen has given Sandro Chia a set of signed photographs and when Sandro and his wife split up, his ex-wife, Paola Igliori, demands a set of signed prints for herself. Victoria is livid; but Allen shrugs and says, "OK." Victoria does as she is told and prepares the order but when Paola comes over to pick up her packet, Victoria curtly informs her that the prints are over on the table and returns to her work.

Allen always makes the gig. He sits with a straight back in his chair. Drinks his honeyed tea. Shakes his arms in the air as he unleashes his poetry in waves of oratory. He needs to be needed. Allen is amply fulfilled by the rapt expressions of engagement in the audience's natural delight. Allen extends himself to their ears. They hear unembellished poetry. Consequently Allen is committed to always giving.

The multiple human complications of life with Peter and Allen continue. Juanita leaves. I engage Victoria Smart. Victoria is a young woman with a phenomenal solitary dreadlock. She is very serious about her work. She doesn't need to be told twice how to do a task. She too cares about Allen. Feels protective about people abusing his generosity. Victoria is on guard against those that would want to double dip into his kindness. We comply with Allen. We aren't always so nice about it. Greedy people piss us off. We also strive with our own petty needs and greedy jealousies.

I find workers to help in the office from friends. Each worker has an area of expertise. Victoria has a special affinity for rock 'n' roll personalities. She is comfortable around them. Jello Biafra visits Allen often. Victoria enjoys hosting. Victoria brings in her friend Vickie Stanbury. Once again I am surrounded by smart women. I am happy.

Allen always has work for us no matter the number of employees. Ted Berrigan calls Allen the *President of Poetry*. Allen detests the idea of being called president. All the while acting like one. He makes sure there is enough work for everyone. If only all presidents could do this! I am spending more and more time on the telephone. Victoria and Vickie are getting the mail. Writing letters. Indexing. Filing. Running to the photocopy shop or post

Victoria Smart and Bob.
Photo by Brian Graham

To Allen, a photograph is a sacred object. It is the friendship inherent in each image that becomes sacred to Allen. Photography is a source of love. Often the portraits are people that he sexually yearns for. I force myself to study pricks of young men. They are usually semi engorged in a limp attitude. An involuntary modesty makes me want to change my gaze. I get the beauty of the hard male body. Allen likes the rippling six-pack and he yearns for the soft lingering of innocence.

The rawness of sacred desire in silver gelatin removes the sexual and leaves only the beauty of attraction. I do feel it even though I get no arousal.

In 1992, Allen actually makes a detailed list poem called *Heart Failure Lovers* (21 pages typed), which catalogs every penis he has ever known. (Are you sweating yet?) His penile vocabulary rivals the Inuits' capacity to name snow!

---

office. Getting things done is what Allen Inc. loves in the world of fellow idiots.

I first see Peter Hale in Allen's photographs. Most of Allen's photographs are portraits of people or his kitchen window. Among the groupings of portraits are young men lying naked on his bed. Peter Hale is in this grouping. He is youthful with curly hair. A toothy grin. Amply cocked. I am normally averse to studying the penis in a photograph. Allen however has a prodigious memory for individual cocks.

What is different about Peter is that he is gay. It pleases me that Allen is starting to hang out with young gay men. Is he tacking away from his proclivity for straight men? Or are young gay men becoming less effeminate? Less affected in demeanor? Peter Hale is emotionally mature and preternaturally intelligent.

Allen asks me if Peter can become part of the office staff. I am a little suspicious. But Peter proves to be both efficient and a quick learner. Peter and I become friends. I become more deeply

I still don't enjoy his explicit gay poems such as *Sapphic Verses*. I assume that I dislike them because they don't sexually arouse me. I ask gay men if they find these poems erotic. Some say, "Oh God! Yes!" and some say, "No Way! They are no more than self-satisfied braggadocio!"

acquainted with Allen's sex life. Even more importantly Peter helps me to understand what it might be like to be gay. I put naive questions to Peter about blowjobs. Anal intercourse. Where and how one is entered. Having this deeper background helps me have more compassion for Allen. I think Allen is always amazed by any attention he receives in bed. Radical amazement is fodder for new poems.

Allen is rich in every way. He has a crazy family. Thieving friends. Intrepid employees. Adoring audiences. He is free of the burden of accumulation. Does this belie the fact that Allen saves everything? No. He does not always treat the archives well. We once found a crumpled set of original Larry Rivers' drawings behind a filing cabinet. They are ruined. I made sure to preserve artists' gifts after that. The value of those art pieces is enhanced by their associational worth. The value of Allen's life grows by his living it.

10 Gay Greybeard

from *Loving Monogamy*

I have had this argument with Allen
he doesn't believe in monogamy
he grows old and his lovers do not
I don't think you have to fuck   different people
to fuck everybody
to grow in pleasure and experience
                mutual growth is synergistic

—————

Whitman slides his hand along your side as he voicifies verses in your ear. Whitman never gropes; there is a true sense of the omni-sexual in Whitman's delicate embrace.

—————

My fatherhood lends me a fragile gravitas, but my non-svelte physique makes me undesirable. It is more likely that Allen is practical and does not wish to chase me away.

—————

Strangely archaic, radically frank, *Message* shocks without hesitation and delivers longings sweet universal straight through my eyes. Sometimes a poem can wake a reader up in a way that the reader never goes back to sleep. Ginsberg teaches the poet to point to one's own shame and joy.

EVERYBODY'S JUST A LITTLE BIT HOMOSEXUAL whether they like it or not. Allen sings this line with a rueful smile. There is never a moment of Allen lusting for me. I am not his type. I am hired after at least one secretary quit after having been chased around the plywood desk. Allen never propositions me. Sexuality for Allen is a mountain he climbs all of his life. At times his views are sublime and other times venal. He helps his lovers and is often wounded by them. Allen is fated to be the champion of the prize but not the recipient.

Allen loves straight guys. This is a common psychological syndrome for queer men of Allen's generation. This recipe dooms one to loneliness. Neal Cassady and Peter Orlovsky are predominantly straight. They make room for Allen in their lives. Allen desires Peter to be exclusively his. However early in their relationship he realizes that Peter is happier with a girlfriend.

Over the years, dozens of "Dear Allen" letters arrive in the P. O. Box after a young fellow's chapbook is published or poetry reading invitation is secured. The writers thank Allen and insist that they will always be friends, but they have to go back to their girlfriends now. Allen takes it with a sigh.

_____

Let's face it!

_____

The essence of American literary tradition explores the line, or lack of, between fact and fiction. Allen is absolutely candid about his sexuality. His persona disarms with a Whitmanic direct appeal to the bodhisattva in each reader.

_____

Allen declaims his homosexuality. His aural *Howl* is a fearless calling out to the assemblage of a new tribe.

When Peter is happy he sexually favors Allen more frequently. While teaching Allen has the chance to meet many young adult men who truly want to please him. Every year at Naropa he has a new lover. Allen opens doors for the young men. Introductions. Parties. Dinners. Gifts. Poetry readings. Publications. Teaching positions. A place to stay when visiting the Lower East Side. Allen and I are standing on Broadway in Boulder. Allen points to the Varsity Townhouses. Muses. "For fifteen years I have had teaching assistant lovers. Now they are a blur to me. I can't remember their names."

Allen is cock driven. A boyish dedication pilots his desires. Makes Allen a courteous lover. Contributes lessons surrounding sexual unions. Buddhist meditation. Poetry composition. Literary gossip. The relationships never last long.

Allen is a gay pioneer. He bravely comes out of the closet long before others even notice the closet. 1959. Allen reads *Howl* at the Big Table reading in Chicago. A lady reporter at the small press conference asks Allen why there are homosexual references in his poetry. "Because I am a fairy, Madam!" Allen camps back in fairy lilt.

I can feel the late 50s shock waves. During the late 70s and 80s I open at least one letter a week from men thanking him. They are grateful to find an open door out of the closet. Interestingly Allen is not a strategist in gay politics. His bravery is a part of his gayness and his poetry. His voice is part of the times. Allen inspires the gay leaders that emerge in the wake of the Stonewall Riots. He does not want to be a gay activist. Allen is much more interested in geo-political matters including covert

"Spy vs. Spy" and COINTELPRO News and underground political magazines grace the pile of reading matter in the little water-closet toilet with pull chain.

———

I realize that being gay is not only about cock sucking and anal engagement. The gay community seemingly flaunts sexuality so that I often hear straight people complain, "Why do they have to show off?" without an awareness of the brash heterosexual branding gays suffer in mass marketplaces. Gay is not as simple as a *padded basket*.

———

As Shelley could sense my wavering, she becomes a deeper attractant to me. I remain immersed in the mature and drawn-out practice of lovemaking.

All sexuality is one.

———

Truly all men are cock driven. Size of phallus in no way dictates the sensitivity to its existence. All men secretly use their cocks to forge new territories. Allen is less secretive about it. He celebrates his cock and homesteads new territories in American Literature through its use.

———

I never get naked or have sex with Irwin or Allen. I only have his sex in his poems. It is precisely this difference that makes my love for Allen pure; I represent his Puritan rectitude. I have become a Hawthornian asset, shaping the world in his Melvilian acceptance of his own desires.

governmental drug distribution.

1980s. GLAD is feuding with ACT UP. Each group calls Allen Inc. to march with them in the Gay Parade. I ask Allen what he wants to do. He is not interested. "You figure it out." This is when I become a professional homosexual. By night I am a straight father. By day I am a gay tactics advisor to the greybeard gay bard. In the end Allen doesn't march with any gay group. He does go to the parade to take photographs.

When I talk to people on the telephone they assume that I am gay. That usually doesn't bother me. I don't want to let anybody down. If I feel there is too much interest in me being evinced by the caller I work in a mention of my wife and children. In fact I sometimes wish myself gay. Most of my favorite poets are gay. James Schuyler. Frank O'Hara. Walt Whitman. Gertrude Stein. Edwin Denby. John Wieners. John Ashbury. Allen. I feel envious of poets with gay sensibilities. I have a deep well of loneliness and domesticity to draw upon. But Steve Hamilton says "Bob you are almost gay! Something went wrong when you were sixteen or so!" I repeat this comment to Allen who adds. "No. It happened earlier."

As befits a Whitman-like Father Greybeard Allen gets sweeter as he ages. He lectures on the gay elements in the *Cadmus* poems by Whitman. Allen's health slows down as do his sexual legs. He can no longer be as physically active. Not as annoying to young men. Now he is approachable as a super intelligent Buddha bear. His self-portrait doodles always display himself as big bellied and naked with a finger pointing to the sky. Do not forget an ample cock dripping drops of essences.

Allen is an innovator in all matters. The obstacles to his

———

The spectacle of the unspeakable is Allen's portal to creativity. His last poems include, *My dick is red hot / Your dick is diddly dot.*

———

Allen is more butch than fairy so his love for straight men makes less sense.

———

Allen's archive has early homosexual literature from the Mattachine Society. He likes to read the NAMBLA Journal. The stories about boys are idyllic and classically erotic. All the contributors use pseudonyms. Allen enjoys it in a rarified conspiratorial air that has no physical expression.

———

A beautiful picture of my son taken by a professional photographer at his music school is posted on the photographer's website. An artist group comprised of adults who were sexually abused as children use Aliah's face on a poster to publicize their art exhibit. They superimpose a whirling red spiral over his face and surround his head with tortured images from the show. To complete the problem, the poster has been pasted up on a wall opposite my son's grade school. I see the posters in the morning and freak out. I scrape them all off the wall before the 3 pm bell. I make a huge fuss with the organizers of the show and they agree to pay a modeling fee to my son's bank account, and to not use the image in the Lower East Side. When I tell this story to Allen, he tells me that I have further abused the artists. I am hurt and angry. Allen could be so dumb when it comes to children! He sees my kid as privileged and these artists as victims. He cannot understand safety under adult protection. He expects the child to pay a price.

love are mostly gone now. Straight men are not his only goal. I adore Allen as a gay pioneer in the straight world. I mix him up with Daniel Boone. He straddles a continent of past *hang-ups.* Takes health risks with illicit love. Allen must be shocking. Allen's relationships are dysfunctional and self-satisfying. He challenges attitudes even in the gay world. And he manifests a deep love for humanity. Sometimes Allen should be emulated by all.

Allen is the herald of queer candor. As such he is less newsworthy as a gay man in the nineties. The societal underbelly where *queers* and *faggots* furtively meet ceases to exist in the "out" world. Allen like his mentor Walt Whitman is envisioned as an omni sexual lover of humanity. Now his sexual truth is safe! Or is it?

Allen joins NAMBLA (North American Man Boy Love Association). This organization promotes inter-generational love through a journal. This smells bad to a father of young children. Allen does not lust after pre-pubescent children. He feels there is a valid freedom of expression issue involved in the NAMBLA journal. He is moved by a high school teacher who writes for it under a pseudonym. This man extols his idealization of young boys. The school discovers his NAMBLA identity. He is fired even though there is no clear record of inappropriate behavior in the school.

Before Allen joins NAMBLA I try to dissuade him. I assure him that I understand his position. I also insist that pre-pubescent boys or girls do not seek out adults for sexual love. Children's true needs are more primary. Food. Shelter. Protection.

Allen feels that his life would be somehow better if an adult man had seduced him at Paterson Falls when he was a kid. "Just

My reply to those who assume that Allen is a pedophile:

Allen is not a pedophile. I work closely with him for his last twenty years and not once do I see, or become aware of, any act of pedophilia. I trust him around my young sons and he never touches them. Allen does believe that the legal age should be made more flexible. And he supports freedom of speech for those who idealize youthful men. His support of NAMBLA Newsletter is to support its right to publish. You can deplore his support but it is not a personal act of sexual deviancy.

————

Allen hates the thought-police and he uses his public persona to be outrageous. He claims that he thinks about making love to *young boys* on noontime live TV in Boston. True or not, Allen wants to irritate a Boston District Attorney who has been busting gays. By staying news, Allen receives a letter years later from the DA's daughter informing Allen that her father was a closet gay.

————

I drive Allen to a gig hours away in a rental car. Irwin turns to me and says, "Don't you think if there was a button to push, or something, to make me straight, that I wouldn't do it; I could marry and have a wife to help clean and cook!" I am touched, but I laughingly tell Irwin that it is too late to find that kind of wife; he'd best stay gay. Later, I ponder why Allen tells me that. I'm not sure if he is sincere. Maybe he is disguising his need for me to stay committed to him.

hanging out." He lets himself be filmed at a NAMBLA event. He is now thought to be a pedophile. It saddens me deeply to witness Allen sully his reputation. He potentially devalues all the important social good he has accomplished. Allen senses my greedy protective attitude towards his reputation. He comically muses to me about NAMBLA. "You know I think I finally found a cause that is completely indefensible!"

Does the iconoclast have to keep casting down the idols until he or she is alone? Allen actually wants to find out. Most of us will never know. We haven't done the transcendent work necessary to support such a lonely position. Allen's NAMBLA membership hinders the offer of a teaching position at his alma matter Columbia University. Denies him poet laureate titles. Bars him from ever writing an op/ed for the *New York Times* again.

Allen's NAMBLA membership is a return to the good fight in former years. He fights sanctimonious prosecutors. Religious or political demagogues (who often turn out to be closeted queens). After all he foresees J. Edgar Hoover wearing a dress in his poetry decades before that truth is known. He builds love into his life that does not depend on orgasms. The love he thrives on is daily gay desire and deep aural transmissions of poetry. That he loves many a penis and only a few vaginas is not as important as the truth that he does love. Within that love there is a Dharma home for himself. His mother. Father. Brother. Bardic friends. Helpers. Each and every bodhisattva on the trail of humanity.

I believe in the early propaganda of the happy gay marriage between Allen and Peter. They make a vow to enter heaven together. Live a life of penury. Peter attacks my family and tries to castrate me. I confess to Allen that I don't understand their relationship at all. I do not blame Allen for loving Peter but I still think he should cut Peter free.

Allen is in no way ready to do that. Peter is a non-negotiable vow for Allen. When Peter slips into alcohol-induced psychosis Allen glows with excitement. For Allen this is akin to the excitement of arriving home after a long absence. He manages Peter's hospitalizations. Doctors. Medication regimes. Bills. Girlfriends. However Allen is becoming less effective at handling Peter's escapades.

Peter has not physically attacked Allen before but he does push Allen down. Allen's knee tendon rips necessitating arthroscopic surgery. Peter and Allen do eventually draw up a legal separation to guarantee Peter's legal right to live in the twenty-four apartment. This means they never stray far from each other.

Sex is harder for Allen because of his numbness below the waist. The rules of engagement necessitated by AIDS slow down the lovemaking process. When he has a new lover they sit and hold each other awhile. Then plan how and in what order they would make love. Allen tells me that the discussion is the best part. Discussing the rules heightens his sexual anticipation. The focus is on more hugging and petting than penetration. It is satisfying and sweet. Ironically Allen Ginsberg once the champion of orgies is now enjoying petting and mutual masturbation as teenagers are so often advised to make do with.

Allen teaches Whitman's lineage to his embracing men in bed. Allen passes on this love and affection to many men. I am a witness in the gay circle. Thus I too am comforted. I can feel the love of brotherhood and sisterhood in this American bardic inheritance.

There is no marriage without a commitment to work to keep the relationship. People are always changing and love changes at the same time. Shelley and I take the normal vows for better and for worse. We didn't know that the *worse* part is not optional. We realize that over time we would go from good to bad and back again.

No matter. Mutual respect avails.

I am proud to work for a pioneering gay organization. But the reality proves complex and I adopt a less naive pleasure in the struggle. I realize that love is every human's right, dysfunctional love included.

I have normalizing wishes for Allen. I love my own marriage and I want Allen to also have a hard but real marriage. Here is the new normal; I wish he finds a new lover that is purely gay and simply pure, and closer to his own age. That there is a gay normal is a light to lessen the darkness of human suffering!

According to Allen, Walt Whitman's coterie embraces the aging bard often in his final years. Get in bed to hug. One man to do so is Edward Carpenter who passes on the Whitmanic brotherhood embrace to Gavin Arthur who later embraces the young Neal Cassady who embraces Allen with both love and sexual comfort.

11 Fame Over Easy

Persona Is To Poetry What A Hero Is To One's Life.

Nothing is wrong with Poetry. Gregory Corso

Poetry saves my life   fills my life with light
I do not see the words but instead hear their echoes
Poetry grows -- loses obscurity -- loses imprecision
at tender and darker moments I turn poems around
before words before sounds before blankness
merge the future in sentient awareness
Persona is clothing become animate

Only time I ever like myself
      is in my persona
poems end breathing out by breathing in!

———
Fame follows one until the day it takes the
lead and then one follows it.

———
Atomic annihilation, degradation of the
environment, the economy of endless war,
taxation of language by war, restrictions on
freedom of expression, declining sentience
among the screen-conditioned public.

IN HIS JOURNAL AT AGE TEN Allen knows that he will be widely known for a literary accomplishment. Does a fifth grader know what a great citizen is? Allen's ambitions remain literary. As his literary power waxes it envelops a poet who feels compassion for all ears. The purpose of his life's work is bettering humankind. Allen balances his desire for recognition by helping to make his friends famous too. He creates poetic drama in which the actors are sacred players. His youthful persona pushes editors to publish his friends. The mature version of Allen beguiles with awareness of global stresses.

Allen achieves sudden notoriety for *Howl*. The stridency of language and oratorical delivery of *Howl* capture people. The true

Eliot Katz suggests that *Howl* constitutes a calling for a new community to emerge from the destroyed tendrils of society. *Howl* enumerates (with "who"s) the members in this community, illustrates the nature of the problem with Moloch, and creates a nascent solidarity with the human progenitor, Carl Solomon, in his plight in Rockland State Mental Hospital.

I notice that only months before composing *Howl*, Allen finds a lifetime lover, Peter Orlovsky, and feels a full flush of joy at being a human being. The poem flows out of him; it gushes his most private thoughts as his love flowers. The poem's hope and solidarity are the twain powerful themes running throughout Allen's life.

———

"Hairy bag of water" is a Gregory Corso expression. Gregory never gets to India although his romantic vision of India makes Allen commit to going there.

———

Early sixties: full beard, beads, long hair, a Benares harmonium, Sanskrit mantras and hand mudras, sandals, mirrored cloth shoulder bag, fringe.

———

I am glad to be given his life work to hold with my hands, and am satisfied as if nothing else brings merits to me; this alone will serve as my obituary. As Allen accumulates accolades, I am unwittingly withdrawing more from my own poetry path.

———

Irwin is horrified if Allen is labeled a prophet.

incendiary content follows its publication. The poem is written to be the least public of poems. It becomes the opposite. Small square copies of *Howl* sit in back pockets and rucksacks as people roam the world looking for truth and beauty.

Allen's new persona does not pop up like toast. No guru whispers a new name to Allen. First he learns. "Don't cling to your visions." Irwin's "hairy bag of water" sits at Calcutta's Nimtala Ghat smoking hashish. Chanting mantras with sadhus as bodies crackle and splatter on the fire. How could one avoid reassessing one's own ephemeral body and temporal persona? Allen becomes his own guru. Returns to America charged with a lifetime's worth of new poems.

Late 1970s. Allen is basking in a television-saturated network. He has well-defined areas of deep interest. He is fearless in expressing political views or social remedies. Allen enjoys a modest level of fame. Low enough that he can walk the streets of New York City freely. He can engage neighbors in conversations without distraction. He can eat in his favorite restaurants. Buy vegetables at the corner fruit stand. Yet he joins the Larry King show when needed by either party. Gets a letter published in the *New York Times*. Allen's deepest media message is the one-on-one interview. While one watches he scrupulously draws in every book. Signs his name into a valueless Burning Ghat called eternity.

Allen doesn't need society's fame as much as society needs him. He needs to be needed. Allen struggles with his need to be important and useful. His spiritual practice detaches ego from his need to please. He needs love from his mother Naomi. His audience and readership supply it. Allen must write about

Allen fully embodies his large persona. This drives him at break neck speed. What a happy coincidence that Allen's need for attention is satisfied by poetry and teaching. His work ethic is exactly at the heart of who Allen is. Allen unflinchingly does what is expected by his persona.

———

He will shatter illusions to do a greater good. One clear example is the Gap advertisement that screams *sell out* to people because Allen seems hypocritical despite that the fee goes to scholarships. This violation is not to be forgiven, no matter the reason. William Burroughs does *sell out* in Nike ads and no one cares. It does not violate William's persona one bit. Allen toughs it out; breathes in the poison and breathes out the nectar. Later, he lets his image be used by Nike; they double the amount when they realize that he is donating all the earnings. He takes unpopular stands without regard for the consequences. He can tame the savage beast within but not always sooth his own readership.

———

Bill's catalog shows me what I had been doing for fifteen years; arranging deposits at Columbia, ending some of the thievery, expanding the size of the files with better clerical efforts, adding new features such as the junk mail poems, nagging the poetry venues to send the required recordings, saving everything but the sandwich wrappers. It fills me with a sense of accomplishment to help hatch this giant egg, which is not only monetarily valuable but also essential for researching the culture of the second half of the twentieth century in America.

———

Robert Creeley's papers are worth ¾ of *a Ginsberg* or *a Ginsberg* could buy both Levertov and Meltzer, etc.

society. He uses prophecy to improve his accuracy. Allen desires enlightenment. Instead finds himself all over again. He enlightens others. Remains satisfied with rare moments of Samadhi. He satisfies this societal need by teaching the principals of Art and Buddhism. Pithy aphorisms on creativity in *Mind Writing Slogans* reflect his desire to make his life useful.

Allen writes *immortality comes later.* In balance his writings and his accomplishments outweigh his failings. Allen is rich by counting the number of people who love him. His fame rests now on his best works. Time will tuck him into the bed of the immortals.

Allen has the entirety of his archives on deposit at Columbia University's Butler Library. The archives are an enduring mirror to Allen's life. Bill Morgan organizes. Catalogs Allen's holdings in excess of 129,000 items. He creates a note card and a discreet number for each item. Bill's catalog greatly enhances the value of the collection. We ask Columbia if they will buy it. They pass. It is rumored that they assume that Allen would bequeath it to them in any case.

Stanford University contacts Bill Morgan about a possible sale. We are anxious to get out of Butler Library at Columbia. The air-conditioning is broken. Precious items are dissolving on their shelves. Stanford's operation is completely climate controlled. Equipped with automated shelving. Allen's archives are the first contemporary literary archives to sell for a million dollars. *A Ginsberg* becomes a benchmark amount paid among librarians. Allen's archives are worth more than a million but no institution will pay more.

The *New York Times* is livid. Allen is portrayed as greedy. The generosity in Allen's purity in financial matters makes his sale seem crass. The accusation angers me because Allen's needs are extremely modest. They are practical to his physical age. Elevator. Grip bars. Bidet. The *New York Times* runs three different articles decrying the sale. One college writing teacher opines that Ginsberg should donate his papers to the New York Public. Allen does want his archives at the New York Public but not as a donation. In any case the timing is wrong. Cash is needed now during Allen's lifetime.

It makes sense to have the Ginsberg archives at Stanford's Library as it is adjacent to the Hoover Institute. That Institute houses the best 1960s underground newspaper collection. Also most of the paperwork of the former Soviet Union. Allen gives half the price to the United States Treasury in taxes. Bill Morgan receives a well-earned archivist/cataloger fee. Our agent gets some. Allen takes the rest. We begin to search for a new home.

He wants an elevator loft with windows on three sides in the Lower East Side. This is a rare combination in our neighborhood but Allen finds it in the *New York Times*! I call the real estate agent for the offering. I hear the description and location. I start to recognize the building in question. I blurt out. "Is that Larry Rivers'

Actually, the Berg Collection at New York Public Library fails to buy the Ginsberg archive because our previous book agent has deliberately neglected to make a full offer. He hoped to break the collection up to maximize the income thus thwarting Allen's deep desire to keep his archive whole.

At first, I can't understand why the *New York Times* is so upset; I come to think it is at heart the old East coast West coast rivalry. Allen belongs everywhere.

The loft for sale is directly below Larry's living area and had been home and studio to Claes and Patty (Mucha) Oldenberg. It is reasonably priced. Allen has enough cash to buy it outright and do a major renovation. I use the knowledge that I gain homesteading to aid Allen. I know an architect that fits Allen's simple needs. The space is open and full of light. Allen requires a clean look with exposed pipes. His only luxury is a bidet in his bathroom. Allen insists that the elevator open onto a mudroom with rugged floor tiles and a bench with shoe cubbies. Allen and I discuss how to create a public entrance that allows both access to Allen's private space and access to the back rooms. I can receive people without disturbing Allen's rest. Allen and his helpers will be united once again.

We floor out an obsolete elevator shaft, I say to Allen that it would make "a great meditation shrine." "Are you kidding? It's a walk-in closet!" Allen orders shelves to be built into the closet. He tells me that he needs room for his sox, his underwear, his trousers, his sweaters, etc. I ask Allen why he doesn't just get "a dresser?" He looks at me with shock, "Why would I want to hire someone?"

Allen designs opaque windows in the walls to conduct natural light evenly to all interior spaces. The last but most interesting Ginsberg addition to the architecture of the loft is the addition of a soup cooling shelf outside the living area window. There are venerable shudder brackets in the brick outside the frame of the window to support the thick Plexiglas shelf. Small holes are added to the shelf to allow rain drainage.

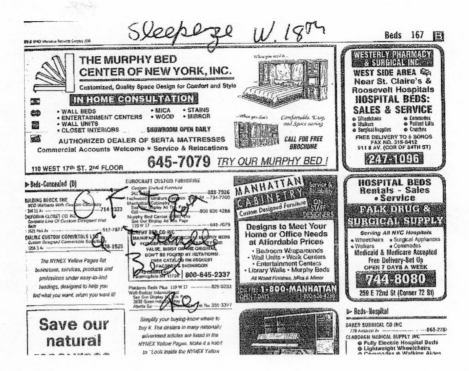

OK I got a Trundle Bed AG

404 East 14th Street building?" It is indeed. Allen calls Larry who is delighted. Larry meets Allen down on the sidewalk in front of the entrance on East 13th Street. As they embrace Larry exclaims. "We will grow old together and push each other around in our wheelchairs!" Allen is happy.

Allen loves shopping for the loft. He visits all the Salvation Army showrooms in Manhattan. Buys a coordinated set of only somewhat worn white leather couches and chairs. He makes a room for Edith. He buys a trundle bed for her visits. We dub it the Edith Room. Poof. All the money is gone.

I love having Allen around more in New York. Allen and I are squeezed together around a center pole in a very crowded rush hour Times Square subway. We cannot move. I see Allen's eyes light up. He says to me. "Watch. No one will listen!" Then he yells at the top of his voice. "It's them Russians and them Chinamen!

133 | Fame Over Easy

Allen and I are coming down Seventh Avenue in a taxi midst crazy midtown traffic. Allen checks out the driver's name and notices emblems and signs that clearly mark the driver as a Moslem. Allen asks the driver if he is a Moslem. Driver says, "Yes." Allen asks what he thinks of Salman Rushdie. Driver is confused. Allen explains about the author that the Ayatollah has sentenced to die. The driver understands and says that he supposed, "If he insults God, he should die." Then Allen turns red in the face and flails his arms screaming, "WELL THEN I SHIT ON YOUR GOD!"

I scream at Allen, "Allen, if you want to get us all killed, do it when I am not in the cab!" Lucky the driver is too busy driving to really understand the fuss.

Those Commies are trying to steal our cars!" Then he repeats this cry. No one responds except to physically try to move a few centimeters further away. Allen stops. We both start laughing.

The Lower East Side is changing. Rents are way up. Fruit stands and mom and pop stores are disappearing. Yuppie becomes a frequently used word. I tell one disgruntled Lower East Sider lamenting the changes not to worry about it. Because "our yuppies can beat up their yuppies!

Allen takes me backstage to meet Bob Dylan. There is a large group seated around Dylan on the floor. Allen introduces me to Dylan. We shake hands. "Bob has been my secretary for more than ten years." Dylan says. "That's a very long time." He gives

Allen is doing a gig at the Bottom Line. It is a Friday in the late afternoon. He has left the office in Union Square slightly frantic and quasi late as usual to catch a cab down to Mercer & 4th streets. "Call them to let them know that I am on my way," he calls back from the elevator. I am used to that and do it. I am closing down the computers and other various humming machines to go home when the phone rings. It is Allen in a state of total panic. "I am an idiot! I was paying the driver and had my wallet in my lap and then leapt out of the cab. My wallet flipped into the street and straight down through a sewer drain! I have got to get it back!" "Can you see it?" "No!" "Can't the guys at the bar help?" "They looked down there but couldn't find it." "Gee, whaddya want me to do?" "OK! (big breath) Call the sewer department and tell them to get over here and lift the drain off. Tell them to bring a crane and some big lights." "Allen, I don't think they'll . . ." "Listen to me! Call them and find out what to do. Oh yes and find out which way the water flows." I realize that this call is going to have to be made. I open the blue pages and get the phone number expecting no answer or a machine. It rings and to my shock a guy answers. He sounds bulky with a Lower East Side accent. I do the common secretary thing, blame the boss, "Hi, well I got a crazy question you see my boss just lost his wallet down the drain and he thinks that you can come over with a truck and lift off the drain and shine lights and get his wallet." "Well, I'll tell what you do. You do just like you would when you was a kid. Ya get some string and some chewing gum and ya lower it down there and pull it up." "Great! I'll tell him." I say, "But wait there's one more thing. Can you tell me which way the water goes? Ya know, where does it go from there?" "Why sure! It flows downstream!"

me a Bodhisattva deep eyeball. I smile. We are all ushered out but Allen is recalled for a private word.

Allen brings Victoria and me to a Grateful Dead concert at Madison Square Garden. Victoria roams off to look for stray kids (lost souls) in the audience. Kids gravitate towards her cool dreads and petite strength. I accompany Allen backstage. He

―――
Allen tells us about a party last night. He meets a singer whom he finds to be really interesting. The singer paints paintings and loves William Blake. The singer knows Allen's poetry. Allen cannot remember the singer's name but he thinks he has heard of him. He goes into the bedroom and flips through last night's journal scribbling. "Tony Bennett! Have you heard of him?" Allen calls, "He says that he would send me a copy of 'White Christmas.'" Sure enough the CD comes in the mail.

Allen likes famous people but doesn't treat them as special. The only famous person that he protects is Bob Dylan. Once Peter Hale listens to Bob Dylan and Allen talk at a small cabaret table. They discuss the people who really control the people who control everything and how many steps away from the real power are Bob & Allen? Peeling back the onion of power leaves one in tears.

―――
I contribute my thoughts; I point out that the Mourner's Kaddish is written in Aramaic not Hebrew. He makes use of it by referring to *the near-Aramaic cantillation of Ray Charles.*

wants to see Jerry Garcia. We run into Bill Graham who greets Allen as if he is a walking oasis. Then a short fellow with a big smile bounds up to us and says "Hi Allen!" Allen asks "Who are you?" He says "I'm Mickey Hart." "Oh are you in the band?" "Yes Allen I am a drummer. I have been in the band since the beginning." "Oh that's nice. Do you know where Jerry is?" Mickey looks hurt. I feel bad. I really love Mickey's world drum music. Although Allen is not a student of fame Irwin can be star struck. Jerry is not to be found.

Allen sits in a public space like a museum lobby. People ask. "Are you Allen Ginsberg?" He replies "No – But that is what I am called."

Allen is clearly aging. He is becoming more and more in demand. People want to hear him read poetry. Sing his songs. They also just want him to talk in workshops and at dinners. Allen now has a laptop computer but he can't use it. I get onto his bed with the laptop across my knees. Take his dictation for the liner notes to *Holy Soul Jelly Roll.* It is harder for me to see Allen now. He sleeps during the day. Goes out at night. Out of town on weekends.

Allen is an icon of the 1940s (the real Beat days). The 1950s (Beat literature created). The 1960s (Anti-war movement/ communal living/chant). The 1970s (Punk/decade of the "wagon": AA   NA   OA etc. and Buddhism). The 1980s (Rise of the neo-cons and their wars. Buddhist teachings). The 1990s. He is approaching his seventieth year. Every social historian or documentary filmmaker needs to talk to Allen. He is a one-stop talking head for the last fifty years. Allen's days are being intensely booked-up as his physical strength wanes.

I place a salutary hope in the new living loft. Allen will have the physical comfort that he needs. The office moves from 12th Street to 14th Street to Union Square. Now it will reunite with Allen's living space again. If Allen has an interview I will be able to manage its length. Bring the interview to its scheduled close. Allen can live a long time. He only has a finite amount of energy left. I see my job as being one that can conserve his energy and mete it out in doses proportionate to the purpose. Only so many readings. Fewer long interviews. Allen's life can be extended indefinitely if I effectively safeguard his energy. Allen has roamed the globe meeting people. Now the world will have to come to him. I have no doubt that they will.

Allen understands his fame. He loves it like a pet. He keeps fame on a leash. Rarely lets it ride him. To counteract his own sense of importance Allen pictures himself as a classic fool. Irwin emerges more often in late night phone calls to old friends. Vain attempts to hang onto lovers. Allen's late poem *Death and Fame* is one of the last great assertions of his persona. He speculates on what his friends will say to each other as they look upon his casket.

> Everyone knew they were part of history except the deceased
> who never knew exactly what was happening even when I was alive.

Deliberately he employs both third and first person. The last line shows that Allen and Irwin are now both with us all the time.

Allen says "first thought best thought." People gasp when they see that he revises his work. He explains that he revises to get back to the original thought. Allen accumulates direct observations and becomes rich. He does not try to control people

Allen folds everyone into history through his poetry; it is concrete and it is abstract. The reader is a listener. When the poet's voice enters the head of the reader, it remains and inhabits the ideas contained in the word objects. Whitman clearly lives inside of anyone who can go the distance with *Song of Myself*. Allen's fans feel his ecstatic rhythms and abject tears and get between the sheets of history with him.

in order to be powerful. He does not need a wardrobe to be well dressed. He needs to be needed by a tender soul. He needs lovers with their complications. This saves him from being a saint. To stay grounded in poetry Allen never forgets his simplest necessities nor does he hide them. His naturalism has the real dirt of living. Allen's huge success gives him enough love to keep him at home in both his body and his life.

12 The Body

The Akedah

for us it is a binding agreement
to live in doubt of own faith
to turn with a helpless eye
up at our creator
not to cry out and not to pray

for under the glint of knife's edge
we lie in direct communion
no angst flows down those rocks
the angel's cry was no relief
there was the perpetual birth
and the unending knowledge
between God and Human

after the professor
spoke so well of Abraham
and whether he passed the test
or no
I was still troubled as always
by this terrible binding
I lay with these thoughts

I recalled my own son
Isaac
born literally laughing
so we named him laughter
I asked a question
to the air around my bed
I asked where in the akedah
is Isaac's name profound?
and so I was answered
the laughter the joy
is in Isaac
it is like wine in a
bottle on a
table
we take wine in
warm with joy
yet the vessel – the bottle
remains on the table
the vessel
the story
        unending

Allen has an *accomplishment body*, completely Type A in all aspects. In fact, he is the Duracell Bunny that intrepidly wobbles forward until a sudden complete collapse. This vessel is cataloged keel to masthead. Each sphere on the tree of life provides a locus to store poems and novels. By living in a map of awareness, Irwin, Allen, and I glow in our wisdom bodies.

HEALTH MAY BE UNDERSTOOD AS SERIAL BALANCING. One must work hard to rest thoroughly. One must eat well but also correctly. One must take in the poison of the world. Breathe out nectar. When I first meet Allen he is strong and vital. I think he has boundless energy. When does he sleep? When does he sit? Does meditation replace sleep? He sleeps fitfully for five or six hours. Lines of poetry punctuate sleep. A journal lies at his bedside ready to receive them. He is wakened by dreams that crawl into his journal.

He rises to shuffle in his sleeveless undershirt and white boxers to the commode to pee. His fishy white feet are laced with blue varicose veins. His legs are slender and brittle looking below his knees. He is slightly bowlegged. His thighs are meaty but not corpulent. They are covered in a fine downy hair that does not make him seem hairy. His penis is average in dimension and shape. He claims that it is bent. I gather that the curvature can only be perceived in an erect state. He blames Alene Lee from an old sexual episode. I am naïve but it seems improbable that any set of muscles could permanently wring a penis into fifty degrees off true. Allen calls it Peyronie's Disease. Alene is a passionate woman. The true source of the curvature is most likely genealogic. A part of Allen's own perception in the fun house mirror of personal modesty.

Allen is fond of his anus. He takes good care of it at the 12th Street office sink. Years of impoverished living abroad teach him to use his left hand. Allen leaves the sink clean. I take some small delight in telling young guests about this as they brush their teeth at the same spot. The reason Allen has to care for his sphincter so assiduously is that he has diabetes caused dysaesthesia from the waist down. This lack of feeling makes it hard to know when to close the sphincter after a bowel movement. This hole remains a source of deep longing for Irwin. He tells me that his penis is now no more sensitive than the bottom of his heel. Because it is thick and insensitive he employs extreme fantasy to achieve a strong erection.

There are a host of problems in his lower belly. He has an appendectomy when a child. Ten years old he tells me. It leaves an

Alene seems like a Jane Bowles character. She is softly full of complacency with smoldering passions. Lucian Carr is one of her knights.

Yes, his asshole is pounded down through years of practice. He likes both bottom and top. Why not?

Extreme fantasy incorporates non-plausible scenarios and the use of imaginary role-playing. Non-extreme erotic fantasy involves the plausible. It rewards true passion.

ugly scar. Irwin says that for a long time after the operation he thinks a piece of his liver is wagging from his side. A relative who is a surgeon performs the procedure. Young Allen never tells any adult about the strange growth. Eventually it dries up and falls off.

When I meet Allen I am surprised to learn that he is having bouts of gout and is regularly troubled by kidney stones. In his case it is kidney gravel. Often he has to pee through a screen to capture the annoyances. He also has gallstones. Eventually his gall bladder is removed. The doctors assume that the gall bladder operation will be routine. It becomes lengthy as they run into a dense layer of scar tissue left over from the septic appendectomy. His stomach and intestinal tract seem to work fine. All the other lower viscera are out of balance.

Surrounding the skull. Skinny neck. Wobbly head. Weak chin. Big mouth. Face half frozen from Bell's Palsy. His left lips turn down in a frozen grimace. The frozen side easily drools so he keeps a hanky handy. His stringy black hair flows off the sides and back of his head. Round black or white glasses sit slightly askew down the nose. Pushed up with his thumb. His beard is trimmed. Sample beard clippings are on occasion slipped into a white letter envelope. Dated for the archives. The wrinkles of his brow smile like the Mona Lisa.

Allen's broad black glasses are as much a trademark for him as his dark curly locks and full beard. His vision prescription changes little. He buys his glasses from Dr. Louie Earle. An elderly gentleman ophthalmologist on University Place. Allen sends many poor poets to Dr. Earle to be outfitted with eyewear. The bills are always sent to Allen. He saves his old glasses. There

———
I think that gout only exists in 18th century novels.

———
He never saves scalp hair.

———
Allen is strong. He holds himself together and marshals all the life forces available to him at every moment: bold youth, ageless guru, levitator, coat and tie professor, Allen embodies poetry and makes poetry out of his body. This worn down strength still straightens out weakness. This physical manifest holds the x-ray shadows of memory.

———
After Allen dies, Andre Voznesenski asks for a pair of these glasses. Allen would not deny Andre, nor do I.

must be a dozen pairs stashed away. Allen often has lovers or friends cut his hair. He does not have a regular barber.

He knows that the beard is the part of his image. People would be disturbed if he didn't have it. During the filming of *Renaldo and Clara* Allen shaves off his beard on camera. He is following a Buddhist principle to break down perceptions and assumptions. Is Allen simply a bearded projection? Well no but what is he without a beard? Allen sees himself as a bearded **Tzadik** (a righteous man). True to his Eastern European ruminations. There is an old proverb that the entire world could be saved if there were just ten true Tzadiks walking the planet at the same time. Ten Allens! It sounds both simple and impossible.

Allen's teeth are in good shape. He brushes and flosses daily and most particularly uses a Stim-u-dent or toothpick to clean his teeth after every meal. Allen is spotted in restaurants with his left hand cupping his mouth as his right hand assiduously pokes around his gums. He does have one broken front tooth whose repair has failed. I recommend my dentist Ruth Simring. He calls her office. Ruth has patients working off their bills by helping her. Allen calls and introduces himself. The amateur secretary tells him that Ruth's calendar is filled. She recommends Ruth's friend and colleague Dr. Lawrence Spindel. When Ruth hears what has happened she has a fit. "I would love to take care of Allen Ginsberg's teeth!" she confides. After that she professionalizes her staff. Allen sees Dr. Spindel who fixes his front tooth for good.

Allen coughs a lot. He is a heavy cigarette smoker. He understands the corporate evil of cigarette marketing through addiction. But it is hard to quit. He quits often during my early years with him. He is always at home on the Lower East Side

Allen goes to India and comes back with a crown of hair. The full beard is his true image. Without beard, he has a weak chin. He looks much more like Irwin.

Decades of smoking cigarettes do not destroy his teeth. No one poison is universal. We need a host of evils to satisfy the body's sins.
Irwin's devils are working in plain view but well camouflaged in benignity.

On his deathbed, Allen sends Dr. Spindel congratulations on having fixed that tooth.

Who lit cigarettes in boxcars, boxcars, boxcars . . .

so he can safely become extremely excitable and irritable. The phone rings. I try to tell the person desperate to talk to Allen that he is not well. Allen sits next to me loudly insists. "Smoking is an illness! I am quitting! It is a valid excuse! I won't talk to anyone!" The caller gets an interesting cacophony out of us. I try to make Allen lie down when he is quitting. He is impossible to be around. I wish he weren't quitting. Of course he goes right back to smoking in a week or two. He has a song or chant called *Put Down Your Cigarette Rag*. He does not perform it when he is in a state of recidivism. This continues on and off for years. Eventually Allen quits forever – almost.

Allen's cigarette battles give him deep compassion for fellow junkies. Smoking does weaken his frame and contribute to his demise; nevertheless the *nine billion dollar capitalistic joke* does not kill Irwin.

Here are Allen and Peter in front of the 12th Street building. They are looking distinctly Eastern European. The photographer is Polish. Allen is beardless with a funny cap on his head. He doesn't usually wear a hat so always looks funny in one i.e. the Uncle Sam Hat or the dark fedora he wore in Synagogue at Aliah's bar mitzvah. Hats make Allen look out of place and important. The boys are dressed up to go out. Allen has his cloth shoulder bag and holds his hand out as if demonstrating existence to existence.

Postcard inscribed by Allen and Peter. Postcard by Joanna Voight.

Allen's outward health is usually robust but he internally carries nagging growing health issues. He has already contracted Hepatitis A in South America in his youth. He also acquires Hepatitis B and C although he does not know how or when. As he ages he develops congestive heart failure. He also develops adult onset diabetes. This contributes to the numbing in his lower half. Brings about his late life adoption of macrobiotic cooking. These are conditions that can be managed by lifestyle changes in diet and repose.

Allen has had two liver biopsies about five years apart. The first one shows some cirrhosis of liver but the later one shows none. He puts the positive biopsy out of his mind.

Allen has many doctors. They like having him as a patient. He is good about going to doctors. Allen loves Dr. Lown's instinctual intelligence and open manner. Allen's cousin Joel Gaidemack is the son of Allen's favorite Aunt Rose He is a physician. I know from Allen that Joel is a gifted diagnostician. Joel's instincts are almost always on the money. He distrusts this doctor. But Allen comes to rely more and more on Dr. Lown.

Allen's health affects me without me noticing. Much of my time is being devoted to making doctor appointments. Picking up medications. Explaining the implications of Allen's declining health to others. This is a sober occupation. The stakes seem high to me. Allen has to be preserved no matter the price. The world needs him. But he is not really a good patient to himself. He will not rest enough. He prioritizes travelling to give poetry readings. If I purposely insert a few free days at home I don't tell him. If he notices the lack of activity he fills it in himself to an even greater degree. I spread his gigs out more. Adding a day here and there

His regular doctor is Shelley Brown, who is also Jonathan Williams' doctor. Allen follows her through various offices and strangely when she retires, he does not engage a general practitioner again. He has a series of cardiologists after that. Dr. Tallury in New York City is very attentive to Allen. Harvey Silverglate recommends his cardio guy in Cambridge, Dr. Lown. Allen tells me proudly that Dr. Lown is a Nobel Prize winning doctor for Doctors Without Borders. Dr. Lown is an intensely simpatico guy and has written a book on the art of listening to patients. Allen and he share the art of listening.

———

This is when Allen becomes most like a father to me. When I get to care for him, my love is clearly defined. There is an increase in authority when it comes to the body. My love will help me stand up to help Allen in his waning.

Allen progresses from hypoglycemia to diabetes. The endocrinologist he sees has a wealthy clientele. He tells Allen that there will be rich meals in Allen's future and for those occasions he can use extra insulin. I ask about problems that diabetics have such as losing digits or going blind. The doctor blandly replies, "Oh the complications! They only happen in about 50% of the cases." Allen and I are not impressed. Next we go to the renowned macrobiotic specialist, Bill Spears. He tells Allen that if he adopts a macrobiotic diet that Allen can go off insulin entirely.

———

True, readings are a mainstay of his income (along with teaching at Brooklyn College) but I keep offering other options to make money while resting at home, such as, signing his photographs or writing articles for thirsty publications. He never does give up the poetry readings. The appreciative applause from young people makes him feel worthy of life the way no other activities can anymore. After a reading tour, he complains that everyone made him the same god damned meal! The organizers sometimes call me to inform me that they prepared the macrobiotic meal for Allen but that he ate off everyone else's plates.

———

June 1, 1995, Allen suffers extreme chest pain. In the hospital, he finds out it is a coronary embolism. Luckily the embolism dissolves without causing Allen permanent damage. This scary event makes me redou-

for rest in the hopes that he won't notice. I start to go to doctor visits with him to take notes. I gird myself for the long haul. Allen's health will become more and more fragile. My ability to manage his good health becomes harder and harder.

The macrobiotic diet is well suited for Allen. The poet Nanao Sakaki teaches Allen a way to make oatmeal with seaweed and tamari. Allen uses that recipe almost every day. The switch to macrobiotics is easy as Allen already owns Japanese cooking utensils. Some fish products are okay. Allen capitalizes on that. Allen has a great love for blue cheese. This is a challenge being both dairy and highly salty. We create new dietary instructions for the hosts of Allen's poetry readings. The instructions include a basic macrobiotic meal that can be easily assembled. Allen is successful in controlling his blood sugar. He is able to get off insulin in a few months.

Allen starts to look frail and skinny. He still roars like a lion when he steps up in front of an audience to orate his poetry. Afterwards he collapses into an exhausted puny heap. Allen will not give up traveling for poetry readings.

ble my efforts to keep him healthy. I determine that I have to alter the power relation between us. I have to boss him around now! Allen's diabetes progresses again despite the change in diet and he eventually has to go back onto insulin. He checks himself with finger prick tests and shoots himself with insulin. As he becomes frailer, I visit a nurse diabetes educator, Jane Seeley, who teaches me how the long-term and short-term insulin work with the body's metabolic rhythm and how to both schedule and shoot Allen with the meds as necessary.

After Allen dies of liver cancer, I wonder why Dr. Lown had not done a hepatic blood work up on Allen earlier. I believe to this day that Dr. Lown understands Allen very well. He knows that poetic creativity is the essence of life for Allen. He is afraid of making Allen less productive as a creative force. Joel thinks Dr. Lown does Allen a great disservice.

Dr. Lown tells Elsa Dorfman that Allen has only six months left to live. Elsa calls me. I am shocked. Does Dr. Lown tell Allen? Allen does not tell me. I don't believe that Dr. Lown tells Allen. Allen cannot keep it quiet. The fact remains that Allen spends the last months of his life writing as many as a half dozen poems a day. Allen gets his fatal diagnosis one week before his final breath. He writes one poem this week. A poem of nostalgia.

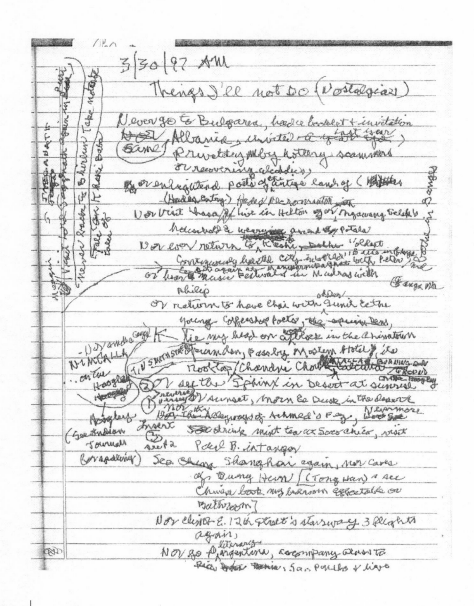

13 Exhale: Let Go

I Slept Through Barchu

I slept through barchu
rose too late to even count
and thought
now must be the final shofar blow
I keened my ears and
heard the ram's horn
blasting bouncing my way
                    and beyond
as sound travels the forest
it is heard but without direction
this forest is somewhere
between my heart and my head

the new year is a clearing
where heart and head can make peace
and hear the way clearer!

28 Elul

Progress Report 7/6/94
Bob: Now on schedule the following
projects --

1. Photo Shows: Tibor DeNagy Venice Bian-
nale 108 Photos Japan 108 Photos Aperture
108 photos 108 photos all of them

2. Books: Selected Poems for Harper,
Penguin, Hanser Germany Italy Saggitario
Maybe France Possibly Spain etc.

3. a. Randy Roark's Blake (I have rough mss.)

b. City Lights Song Book (complete Songs)
(Waiting on Steven Taylor to re-do music)

c. correspondence (Miles)

d. essays (Morgan/ Rosenthal)

e. interviews - David Carter

f. Mind Writing Slogans handbook-- Jacqueline Gens

(2) *Progress Report*

*I also have backlog of 2 years unreturned
Term papers – NYU, CUNY, Bklyn.*

Allen

———

Eileen Myles describes Allen's poetry as
remarkable for its trailing lines of details.

———

There is a prevailing feeling among critics
that Allen writes his best poems in the late
1950s and consequently the later work is
not noteworthy. I think this is a critically
irresponsible argument for its inherent
laziness.

———

Allen memorized Khlebnikov, Mayakovsky,
Essenin, Baudelaire, Milton, Wordsworth,
Blake, Whitman, Swift, Dickinson, Rimbaud,
Williams, Pound, etc.

———

Ted Berrigan tells me that one judges an
artist by their best work.

ALLEN NEVER LOSES HIS STRIDE. Even though he is weaker
in body. Summer 1994. His mind races to plan all the projects
that still lie ahead of him. He writes into his journals daily. He
reads new books on fiscal policies. New fact details flow into his
poetry. William Carlos Williams praises *Bricklayer's Lunch Hour*
for its direct vision and plain diction. Allen continues to put
plain American speech into deceptively simple poetry that never
backs down. Allen's poems change scope and intent but do not
diminish in quality. It is clear that Allen writes a lot and his work
is uneven. This is true from the very beginning. Allen's poetry
always creates life as poetry. Each novel enjambment of words
passes through a filter of the western canon. This is the secret
of the freshness to his verse. He also uses his ears to direct the
diction. He hears patterns in all speech. Saves those patterns for
his poems. He reads all of his poems dozens of times before they
are published. Hearing himself recite a single poem repeatedly
refines his aural acuity in the lines. He always has a pen ready
while he gives a reading. Notates as needed before turning his
page. A black fountain pen is handy to do his bidding. In addition
to pedigree and diction Allen finds new ways to make each
poem's conceit engage the reader. I marvel at his delicacy of

candor. There is beauty in truth that never leaves Allen's line. He doesn't open new worlds to me. He opens my eyes to the world I find myself in.

Allen is committed to doing every interview request. He does many benefits for causes. His calendars are filled. His Allen Inc. workers in the office doggedly persist with business arrangements. Artistic tasks. Travel particulars. Peter Orlovsky stays an active case for Allen. Allen outlasts all of Peter's girlfriends.

Allen's slowing down is not yet perceptible to the larger world. Traveling continuously. Schlepping his harmonium case and book bags. He is out of breath. Both congestive heart failure and diabetes threaten his life. Treatment demands that he stay home and rest. He covers up fatigue and pain with a narcotic. After extending his energy a few days with the painkiller Allen collapses moribund for a day or two. His sleeps grow deeper. Longer and more frequent.

Teaching at Brooklyn College is a concession to his slowing down. When he travels to read poetry he enjoys the open faces of young people with their ears cocked for his voice. At Brooklyn College he holds the class in rapt attention without the hassle of flying. Although I do not always sit in on his classes I help him organize his Rainbow Poetry Series and attend them. John Fisk gets into cabs with Allen to record the readings. John is a sound engineer and radio personality. John loves Allen and collects Ginsberg publications. Before one of the readings Allen asks: "Is it rolling John?" John treasures that bit of tape. Although Allen can teach poetry as effortlessly as falling off a log he has a horrible time grading papers. He often has students over to his apartment for soup and a chance to talk. One orthodox Jewish student in a black hat privately confesses to Allen that he is gay.

Think Bob Dylan -- *Nashville Skyline*

I meet this man years later. He has come out gay but has to leave his black hat behind.

148 | Straight Around Allen

The young man brings his buddies over to Allen's house. They sing ecstatic hymns all through the night. Allen is enraptured.

Allen begins to cancel classes at Brooklyn College. He is too exhausted to teach. The poet Joan Larkin covers for him. He takes trips up to Boston to see Dr. Lown. Stays with Elsa Dorfman and Harvey Silverglate. Elsa prepares macrobiotic food for Allen. Later hears Allen at 4AM rummaging through the refrigerator "eating the treif" as Elsa puts it.

September 1996. We move Allen into the loft before it is finished. He loves it. He loves the elevator. He loves the muscular young men working in the space without shirts. If one of them hurts a finger Allen is right there with some good drugs.

The office moves out of Union Square a month later. Now occupies the rear of the loft space. I hire friend Lori Johnson to be Allen's housekeeper. Lori comes by every day with her young son Cullen. Allen happily gives her a shopping list and money. Lori shops and cleans as needed. She lives close by so that she can pop in for short visits. We have the phone number for a Lower East Side limo driver who is available to drive Allen. Peter Hale efficiently manages the files and paper flow. Puts the ever-growing numbers of papers into a logical order. Peter also does most of the typing for Allen including the first typing of poems out of Allen's journals. I train to help administer Allen's skin tests and insulin dosages. I think that at long last we have Allen's affairs in the best order. For the first time I actually know what I am doing. But the problem with perfection is that it does not hold. Indeed Irwin Allen has a different agenda.

He has a beautiful living and workspace. We have the best and most complete staff including a ready driver.

This is my earliest writing about Allen's last days. I send it to Allen's biographers for their possible benefit. I am leaving it mostly intact to maintain its tone of immediacy.

Denouement

Allen was unsteady on his feet. Hesitant in his step and exhausted in his frame. He had to fly the shuttle to Boston to visit Dr. Lown in Cambridge the next morning. For the first time, I sensed that he didn't have the vital energy to fly by himself. "Allen, I'll go with you." I reassured him in the early twilight of a late afternoon, February 24, 1997. He protested that it was not necessary. I insisted and he gave in happily.

I had never seen him unable to get out the door before. My whole life was changing; moreover, an era was dying.

I carried my bag and his. He shuffled with me. The morning sky was dark and threatening. In the taxi to LaGuardia Airport, Allen asked for his book bag. Street lamps whisking by in an alternating stream lit the taxi. As the vehicle sped back and forth between lanes, I felt my stomach rising up to my throat. Allen said, "Listen to this. I started it last night!" He was laughing and cracking up. He searched his bag and found the journal with the scrawled poem. It started "When I die I want the biggest funeral…" I wanted the cab ride to be over fast. It was hard to listen to the poem but it got funnier and funnier. He was almost in hysterics as he listed what all his myriad of boyfriends would say at his funeral. He wanted to know if I could add any lines. I suggested the women would all say, "He never did remember my name."

On the shuttle aircraft, Allen fell into a deep sleep. I stared at the deep lines in his face. He seemed so far away. I thought he might be dead. But at the beginning of our descent, he jerked awake and grabbed his notebook and scribbled for about two minutes and read me this American Haiku:

"My father dying of Cancer, head drooping, oy kindelach."

Elsa dropped us off at Dr. Lown's offices in the morning. I read Dr. Lown's book on patient care as Allen waited to be seen. Dr. Lown examined Allen and had blood drawn. I was invited in on the conference. Basically, Dr. Lown wanted Allen to stay close by to monitor his medications and possibly do further tests. Nothing in the physical exam alarmed Dr. Lown. Allen was eager to share "Death & Fame" with him. The doctor was amazed at Allen's humor and clarity. Death was in the air but it didn't seem to stick to anything. We taxied back to Elsa's and Allen lay down to rest. I decided to return to New York City for Elsa and Harvey would take great care of Allen and were honored to do so. As Allen slept, Elsa told me how Allen had gotten up in the middle of the night and eaten the *tref* again.

Now we entered the arena of make-believe. "Everything will be all right." "It's just the new medication." Allen stayed at Elsa and Harvey's several weeks. I canceled the several classes at Brooklyn College. Peter Hale and I fielded scores of calls about Allen every day. Some wanted health updates. Many people wanted to schedule time with Allen and many had unfinished projects involving Allen that they were starting to sweat about.

I resolved to get Allen a new medical team all based at Beth Israel Hospital, located two blocks away and visible from Allen's new bedroom window. When I talked to Allen in Cambridge, he sounded weaker than when I had left him. The suspected medicinal culprit had been stopped immediately but it had a long presence in the system. It would take weeks to clear. We were told that Allen had hepatitis and increased liver fatigue as a reaction to the pulmonary medication. I requested an emergency leave of absence and Joan Larkin was engaged for the next four weeks.

We were still in boxes. Bill Morgan was shelving Allen's books and making bookplates for the categories. I was having more shelves built by Ned Lindsay, grandson of Vachel Lindsay. Lori was keeping the loft clean. Joey Golden (Lori's husband) was cleaning all the white leather couches, which Allen had bought at the Salvation Army. The loft was complete. So much work had gone into it. The renovations were complete. Allen would have it all: a bidet, a housekeeper to shop and clean, and an elevator to end the slow trudge of tenement days. Allen eagerly awaited a visit from his stepmother, Edith, and wrote her name upon its door. Here was Allen with a great staff in a great place in the first home he owned that was really for himself.

Allen was strong enough to fly by himself. We worried in New York and Elsa fretted in Cambridge. Allen arrived and buzzed us to help with his bag. We rode up the elevator and he took to his bed. Allen's cousin, Dr. Joel Gaidemack, visited. He had always advised Allen on his health as Allen saw cardiologists, endocrinologists, Tibetan doctors, acupuncturists etc. He was furious with the Cambridge cardiologist. He pointed his finger at me and ordered me to get Allen "hooked" into Beth Israel. I promised that was the next move.

The first week back from Cambridge, Allen progressively weakened. He came home in time to see Steven Taylor and his wife, Judy, with their new son. He was so glad that he made a huge vat of fish chowder. He sent Lori out for fish, fish heads, clams, mussels, and a massive assortment of vegetables. He called Shelley to get advice and started to throw the soup together. I was weary of it. He didn't seem to be washing things well and the shellfish went in still in their shells. We all had to taste it and admire it. Then the huge pot was put out to cool on the new shelf. Visitors at that time included Robert Hunter and his wife; Andrew Wylie came for lunch. Allen would be up for a few hours and then to go back to bed. He was writing a lot of poems into his journal. Allen actually got himself to his last reading. On March 9, 1997, he was the featured reader at a slam at New York University. He admired a young NYU poet, Beau Sia. He read and heard the rest of the slam and he hoped that Beau would study voice techniques so that his high speed, high volume frontal assault on his poetry would not leave him without a voice.

For two weeks Allen got weaker and on a Friday in mid-March he was having such a bad day that he just couldn't get out of bed. He lay on his side groaning. Waves of nausea wafted through him when he had to move his bowels and the urge came often. I called Joel and told him the situation. He said, "Bob, get him in the Hospital now! His systems are failing and he'll be dead in twenty-four hours!" I had to get him into Beth Israel where we had not yet found new doctors. A friend of mine was a nurse there. I called Barbara Glickstein up and told her my fix. She made some calls and called me back and told me that she had spoken to the head of cardiology who was leaving for his home before Shabbat. But the doctor did call me and explained that his colleague would be there and we should bring Allen into ER and they would be waiting for us. Bill Morgan went to the Key Pharmacy down the street and rented a wheelchair for $5. Allen protested the chair but I insisted and he acquiesced. He managed to put his grey parka on and his grey knit stocking cap and sunk into the slightly crummy wheelchair. I pushed Allen and Bill opened doors. It was just three little blocks to the Beth Israel ER. I wheeled him up

———

Judy Hussie-Taylor and their son Eamonn.

to the triage window, and spoke to the intake person who told us to wait. Allen peered at me forlornly amongst the other patients awaiting treatment. Then in two minutes we were called in and Allen transferred to a hospital bed in ER. Bill took the wheelchair back to the pharmacy. I did Allen's intake paperwork while he was being hooked into a heart-monitoring device. Allen was so relieved to be under intensive care that he held my hand and thanked me for "engineering a little miracle."

Later that evening as Allen was brought to a room, an ER doctor had shoved a poem into Allen's hand while he lay on his gurney. Allen awoke in a large bright room he had all to himself. He was getting VIP treatment. Fresh fruit was delivered to his room. From his window, he could see his bedroom window in the new loft on 14th Street. I didn't know who the admitting doctor would be for it had not been determined why he was deteriorating so fast. When the cardiologist came up, Allen handed her the poem, which he had marked up with major editing notations. He asked the doctor to return it to the ER physician. She was surprised and said, "That was kind of rude of that doctor." Allen broke into a self-satisfied smile and said, "I made it a much better poem."

The weekend was slow but some cardiologic tests were run. On Monday, the hepatologist, Dr. Clain, would visit. I made sure to be there. I had brought three huge file folders full of Allen's medical papers including test results, x-rays, and letters from the office. Dr. Clain was soft-spoken with a South African accent; he sat on the edge of the bed. Allen was dozing. I rifled through the fat folders and found the results of Allen's first liver biopsy in 1989 at Lenox Hill Hospital. They had found evidence of cirrhotic scarring. Yet a liver biopsy done just three years later at Bassett Hospital, Cooperstown, New York, failed to show liver disease. Allen's liver had been first injured when he was in his twenties in South America by contagious hepatitis. I related a brief history of the following years: kidney stones, gallstones, periodic bouts with gout, spleen removal. Then I mentioned Allen's childhood botched appendectomy. I related that Allen had told me that after the operation, he had thought there was a piece of his liver sticking out his side. It finally dried up and dropped off. When I had first heard that story, I was struck how he as a child had no one to show his wound to. Dr. Clain said it must have been severely infected. He examined Allen's torso and said indeed there had been a serious infection. "So Mr. Ginsberg, this happened when you were a child?" Dr. Clain asked. "Oh No!" Allen piped up, "I wasn't a child. I must have been ten!" I wept to myself. Allen hardly had a childhood.

Allen gained some strength and Peter Hale and I visited with him every day. He wanted a special phone book made for him comprised of the best numbers for his closest friends. I recalled my earliest days and the appellation "Cream File." At first, he needed ten names and numbers. Each day he asked for more. Each day we re-alphabetized the list and brought it in and each day, he scribbled down more names to put on. He also gave us four or five new short poems to type and bring back for his changes. Meanwhile in the loft, we struggled to get Allen out of boxes. I was to be taught how to shoot Allen up with insulin but events overtook us. The next day held a liver biopsy for Allen. We knew that would be hard on him.

Allen continued his phone calls and met with doctors. The liver biopsy happened and I was relieved that Allen felt fairly strong after it. We continued to plan Allen's homecom-

Here is the tragic flaw: The dislocation of childhood and the weakening of the main frame.

ing and make his home perfect. We finished unpacking and cleaning on Friday about noon, and then decided to have a feast from the Mee Noodle shop just across First Avenue, which Allen adored. Allen loved the whole flounder in ginger sauce and it was one of the dishes we ordered. Joey, Lori, and Cullen were there. Bill was there. When we were almost done eating and feeling jolly after the frantic work, the phone rang. Peter picked up the cordless phone in the kitchen. It was Allen. He sounded different. His voice seemed more tentative. He asked Peter if the poems that he wanted typed were ready yet. Peter replied "Sorry, not yet." Allen became agitated and said that they must be typed at once, "Drop everything else and get them ready!" Peter was disturbed by this unusual stridency. Allen asked to talk to me and Peter handed the phone to me as he walked toward the street windows pondering this new voice. Allen told me that he got the results of the liver biopsy, "It's cancer. It's not operable." I said, "Oh Allen!" I told him that I'd run over soon and I told him about the loft being ready and the feast. "Oh, the flounder, that's good!" he said.

When I hung up, I went back to the office without speaking to anyone and shut the door. I sat at my desk and put my head down on my elbows on the plywood desk. "It has come to this!" I stepped back into the kitchen and asked Peter Hale to come back. I shut the door again and told Peter exactly what Allen had told me. We hugged and said nothing. I told Bill. Peter swiftly typed up the poems before he and I went to see Allen.

Allen was alone in the lovely bright late March afternoon. Peter and I came in and I sat down next to his bed and put my hand down palm up near his chest. His right hand came down and squeezed my hand hard. He told us about Dr. Clain's visit. Dr. Clain said that the cancer had heavily metastasized and that no operation was indicated. He told Allen that he might have four to six months to live from onset but that the date of onset was very unsure. I was Allen's health proxy and we talked about the next moves. Dr. Clain recommended the Hospice Service at Beth Israel. Somehow we managed to keep it businesslike. I think Peter was quietly weeping.

Allen and I talked about a projected book of essays, and about Peter Orlovsky; Allen wanted to be nursed at home by Peter. I told Allen that I would come back to continue the conversations about the various projects left to finish. Just about then, Anne Waldman and her son, Ambrose, came in. Peter and I solemnly said hello and told Allen we would be back the next day. Allen did not want us to tell anybody about the fatal diagnoses. He couldn't be discharged into hospice till later the next week. He called everyone and told them himself. One of his very first calls was to his ninety year old stepmother, Edith, whom he had so desperately hoped would come to live part of the year with him. On Saturday, I brought my sons, Aliah and Isaac, to visit Allen. I asked Isaac to bring his camera to shoot Allen. Allen was happy to look into the young man's camera. He sat up for Isaac and, as he always did, made the shoot good.

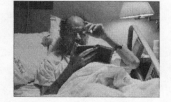

Photo by Isaac Rosenthal

Allen continued to make calls. He cried with people and made deathbed requests of rich men. Allen laughed, "They can't refuse me!" He felt pretty good and imagined that he had several months to live. He wrote his last poem in hospital; it was a poem of nostalgia. Peter and I went to pick Allen up on Wednesday morning. Many of the hospital staff and doctors were coming by the room to say good-bye. Allen read aloud his last poem, "no more evenings with Oz on Ocean parkway." Peter couldn't understand who Oz was and stopped Allen's reading. Allen was annoyed, "Oscar! Oz! My cousin Oscar Janiger. No more evenings with Oz on Ocean Parkway!" I had brought the hospice wheelchair. Allen slipped on his grey winter parka and his grey knit stocking cap and got in for the short push home. I pushed Allen. Peter Orlovsky took a roll of pictures on the short walk.

Allen was very happy to be home at last. The loft seemed perfect with Allen in it. I asked him if this was not a lesson in impermanence and to my surprise he answered, "No, I intend to enjoy this place to its fullest! I will take a safari to the water cooler." Allen rested a bit and then got up. We put the new diabetes and food schedule into action. Lucien Carr dropped by briefly to say farewell. He had to go quickly so as not fall apart emotionally. In the afternoon, Lori and Cullen came over to clean. Allen told me that he wanted me to set up a full recording studio in the loft. I was already scheduled to buy a new piano on Friday. The purpose was to be ready in case Bob Dylan or Paul McCartney came to visit. Lori was cleaning up as the day started to darken, sending its Western orange light beams across the floor. Shelley came over with a chicken to make chicken soup, the steadfast cure-all. Peter Orlovsky came back to move in and nurse Allen. "You don't know how good he was to my father as he lay dying." "Yeah, twenty years ago." I thought. Robert Frank came over. He was sweet and quiet as always. He had a new catalog of his work. He signed it for Allen and mentioned Shelley making soup and Lori cleaning in the flyleaf. Allen took a picture of Robert and Peter at the kitchen table. The atmosphere was warm and loving. Allen was bright and cheerful. Later Allen had his soup and I left him in Peter's care as was his dearest desire.

I came early on Thursday to start Allen's schedule. He told me that Peter didn't stay with him because Peter needed to smoke and sleep with windows open. Peter also had to watch television. He set himself up in Edith's room. Allen told me that he had showered but Peter hadn't helped. Instead Peter took more photos. None of that bothered Allen but it utterly unnerved me. Peter came into the kitchen where Allen was sitting. Allen asked me if I didn't think that Peter should trim his beard. I forced myself to be pleasant and said, "No Allen, Peter looks fine. He looks like Brahms!" Allen liked that. This was the day Allen had decided that we should release the news of his cancer. We drafted a simple statement and sent it to the U.P.I. and the *New York Times*. Allen went back to bed saying that he did not feel as well as he did the day before.

In the afternoon, Fernanda Pivano called. She had Ettore Sottsaas on the line. Allen had been desperate to reach Ettore. Reluctantly, I went to wake Allen. I whispered that Ettore was on the line and asked if he wanted to take the call. Allen weakly nodded yes. As he shifted to prop himself up, he started puking. I had the wireless phone in my hand as I reached for a towel to help Allen clean up. Allen said, "This hasn't happened before!" He had previously felt intense nausea but had not puked. I told Nanda that unfortunately that this was a bad time. She got excited and demanded to know what was happening. I couldn't think of what to tell her and just said that Allen needed my help and hung up on her and Ettore. Allen made it to the bathroom after refusing my arm. He came back to bed and went into a deep sleep. Later in the afternoon, I decided to get a haircut. Peter was around. I had to give him another chance. Peter Hale helped Allen get up to go to the bathroom. When Allen came out, I was about to leave for my haircut. I asked Allen if he was going back to bed. "Oh Yeah." he intoned with great weariness. When I

Surrounded by a loving care system, Allen gets into his own deathbed; exhilarated and awaiting the hoopla.

came back, Allen was still asleep. I reviewed the schedule with insulin and meals with Peter and sternly told him to call me later. "Peter, when Allen coughs, check his breathing to make sure he is not choking himself to death." "Oh that can happen?" "Yes Peter, you have to be here and be on your guard." Later at 10PM, Peter Orlovsky had not yet called me so I called over but no one answered. I pondered running over. But again, I told myself that this is what Allen wants most in his life now. Allen wants to be alone in the night with his "nighest lover."

———
[Note I placed on the refrigerator]
Thurs 4/3/97
Peter [Orlovsky]
Allen needs to do finger Stick Take 6 units Insulin Lactulose 5 Tablespoons & Glucotrol -- Help him to Eat early & Late.

Bob

Thurs 4/3/97
Peter
Allen needs
To do Finger Stick
Take 6 units Insulin
Lactulose 5 Tablespoons
+ Glucotrol -
Help him
To Eat early
+ Late.
Bob

I awoke extremely early Friday morning. I called Allen; no one answered. I called Bill and we decided to head over to the loft together. We arrived at the loft about 7:30 AM. I opened Allen's door and we walked forward all the way to his bed. Allen was asleep with his head cocked to his right. He seemed different. His breath was stentorian. I gently called out, "Allen." No response. I put my hand on his shoulder and repeated his name. Still there was no reaction. Gingerly, I shook him. No response. I got scared and ran to the office to call the hospice service. I told the nurse about Allen's deep sleep. She suggested that I vigorously shake him and call her back. I went back to Allen with resolve and gave him a firm shake and strongly called out, "Allen! Allen! Allen!" No reaction! I walked back to the office with a growing dread in my heart and called the service. She said that she would have the doctor call. He called soon and I described the situation; he said that he would be right over. I walked out of the office and then found Peter O. He had a mountain bike in the hall. "Where did this come from? " I asked. Peter said that he had bought it on the street last night. "How much do think I paid, Bob?" "Well, they're about three or four hundred new." "Well, I paid three hundred dollars!" "Why Peter?" I was bewildered by everything. The thought of the dysfunctional, rotund Peter on a bike didn't make sense to me. I realized that he was out last night buying this bike when he was supposed to be watching Allen. I asked, "Peter did you realize this bike was stolen? What's the karma for buying something you know is stolen?" "Gee Bob, that's a good question; I should find out!" He went back into Edith's room to smoke. I forgot to tell him about Allen.

155 | Exhale: Let Go

I stood alone breathing. My world was ending and was yet still far from beginning again. Called Eugene and told him that his brother was dying. I called Edith and told her that her stepson was dying. I called Gelek Rinpoche in Ypsilanti, MI. and told him that his sangha member was dying. He said that he would fly right out. I called Philip Glass and told him that his friend was dying. Bill Morgan took over the job of calling people. He called Peter Hale. Hale had just woken up and heard the news on the radio about Allen's incurable cancer. He was standing still in a mild state of shock when Bill called. "Peter, I think you had better come in fast."

Philip Glass came over and sat with Allen. I realized that soon many people would come over. The nurse came and I welcomed her and set her comfortably at the foot of Allen's bed. She stroked Allen's head and talked to him. "They like to be touched and talked to," she said. Eugene came. Joel came. I was in a strange daze. The loft filled and Allen was caressed and purred to all day. I asked the nurse if there were too many people around Allen. "Oh no, there can't be too many. Don't worry."

The loft filled with artist friends, sangha friends from Jewel Heart and Shambhala, Peter Orlovsky was agitated and disappearing to smoke cigarettes. Gregory Corso held a small circle around him. There was a chair pulled up to Allen's side and people took turns sitting with him, holding his hand, and talking to him. People were comforting and composed. Gelek Rinpoche arrived in the early evening with Kathy Laretz and three monks. They huddled over Allen and then Rinpoche spent some private time with Allen. After that, they set up their chanting at Allen's altar. The room filled with the low tones of chanted Tibetan scriptures with the occasional rattling of instruments. Joel marked Allen's progress. Then George and Anna Condo ordered Chinese food in. Shelley and our two sons, Aliah and Isaac, came in and held Allen's hand. Isaac heard Eugene's parting words to Allen. Isaac came back to the office and told them to me. I made him write them down, "Good night Little Allen. I'll see you soon." Late in the evening many people showed up from the Shambhala Center. This day was the tenth year anniversary of Chöygam Trungpa Rinpoche's death. There had been a gathering to mark that event. I discussed the funeral plans with Charles Lief and David Rome. At one point we had a conference with Rinpoche and it was decided that the funeral would be at the Shambhala Center but that Rinpoche would preside. Rinpoche explained to me that it was very important that after Allen's final breath that he not be disturbed and that no one touch him. Gelek Rinpoche gave Peter Hale a special liquid to place on Allen's lips after the last breath. This would constitute Allen's last food. People started to drift home around midnight. We had no idea how long Allen would remain. Rinpoche and monks were beat and Rinpoche figured that Allen would still be here at dawn. They went to sleep at nearby Philip Glass's house. Patti Smith and Oliver remained. Rosebud Feliu and Simon Pettet remained, Joel stayed. Bill never left the office. He handled the phones tirelessly. Gregory went home demanding to be called if anything changed. The loft got quiet and people found couches and chairs to sleep in. Joel and I lay down on Allen's platform bed just a few feet from Allen's hospital bed. I slept for a few minutes at a time. Joel checked Allen's pulse and said that the pulse was slowing and "it" would be this night. At about ten minutes after 1 AM, Allen made a noise. He groaned and his torso jerked. The nurse checked him and Joel did likewise. Joel said it was a seizure and that the end was rapidly approaching. Twenty minutes later Allen gasped a low guttural groaning exhalation as his body jerked upright a bit. His head rolled further to his right and his eyelids lifted. His eye rolled and stared directly at me. I gazed into Allen's eye and could discern that the eye was devoid of sight. Joel stood near Allen monitoring his breaths. "It's coming fast now!" We gathered around Allen in stony reveries. I was cross-legged on Allen's captain's bed in complete attention. Allen's breath slowly wound down. Peter Hale got ready to deliver Allen's last food. He looked at Allen intensely. I prepared myself to say the Sh'ma and I was nervous. The breaths came further apart. Joel said, "This is the last one." There was one more. Joel hesitated this time and waited a second. We all knew "it" had happened. Allen passed from the gross sphere of the living; there was not even a shudder in his body. His last breath spread out into the room and never returned. Peter Hale used the eyedropper to drop the food on Allen's lips. The food was red. I put my hand over Allen's eyes and haltingly called out, " Sh'ma Israel, Adonai Eloyhenu, Adonai Echad!" Listen people, the Lord is our God, the Lord is One. How Allen had vociferated in the world with tongue of fire against the one God! How pleased he would be to be treated as one of the tribe! The time was one thirty-one in the morning, April 5, 1997.

Rinpoche said that Allen was not ready to move yet. He explained that certain changes would happen and then he would know when it was OK to move the body. People started coming over again. The chanting continued. Bill manned the phones. Peter started to show signs of cracking. We roped Allen off and put up a sign on the rope, which read, "Please pay your respects from here." Allen looked peaceful. There was no strain in his face. I opened the windows behind him to the cool April breeze to keep him fresh.

The whole day was a blur of sleeplessness. I contacted the funeral home and made the arrangements for Allen to be picked up in the early evening as I had figured sixteen hours would be enough for Allen to devolve his mind in his death samadhi. When I talked to Rinpoche in the late afternoon and he took me to look at Allen, he mentioned that there would be a hollow dimple forming at the top of Allen's cheek to mark the start of the final phase. There was no dimple yet. I called the funeral home back and put them on hold.

Bill was strained to the utmost. He babbled incoherent things to me and I urged him to sleep here, not to go home. Bill went home and I worried he would attack anyone who looked at him cross-eyed. I called his house till he answered. I thanked him and praised him. I'll never know how much he did. I'll never be able to fully appreciate how much weight he took off me!

Peter Hale hit the end of his rope and went home. Peter Orlovsky was trying to get people to take books home. "Rosenthal will send them to Stanford on Monday!' he said as he pressed books into people hands. Mostly they just put them back when Peter wasn't looking. At about 11 PM, the hollow dimples appeared in Allen's upper cheeks under the eyes. Rinpoche said I could call the funeral home now. There were still thirty or more people in the loft. They wouldn't go home till Allen left. The men came and I led them to Allen. People gathered round but I requested they all back off except for Peter and me. Peter held his hands together in a devotional attitude his mala beads wrapped around his fingers. As the men prepared to lift Allen onto the gurney with the body bag,

Peter Orlovsky is not leaving. I can't talk to him. Rani Singh offers to sleep in the loft and thus guards the library.

I held a white Buddhist scarf, which I thought to place around Allen's neck. I looked to Rinpoche and he nodded approvingly. Allen was zipped up and wheeled out and at a little past midnight people went home. Allen had spent twenty hours in samadi. He was a highly evolved meditator and there were complex mental gyres to unwind. Shelley and I went out into the cool night air. As we walked by Tompkins Square, I heard the bell-like voice of Martin Luther King in my head. He rang out, "Free at last. Free at last. Thank God Almighty, Free At Last." We stopped and looked at a huge plume of white vapor arising from a manhole. A street lamp behind a tree caught the steam in frozen poses broken by the black limbs of the boughs.

14 Lost & Found

Advice

the young man stood reproving me:
you see this is the age of the asshole
you have to be an asshole to get ahead
everyone is an asshole
I had to learn how to be an asshole
then I had to learn how to be a bigger asshole
I have a master's degree in asshole
the only thing you can trust
is that everyone is an asshole
you didn't teach me to be an asshole
your friends aren't assholes
those old beat soldiers saw the asshole as an old comrade
the academic old men gloried in the products of the asshole
reams of old man shit fill the libraries
Dr. Williams would say today that
there are a lot of assholes out there
the wrinkled hole, the nether eye, the backdoor, the crab like joker,
    no talent   texting driver   parking space grubber
    the one your lover always leaves you for
    bully neighbor
if you are not an asshole – you are an asshole
it takes one to know one
I am learning to be a real hole in the ass
your ears are little hairy holes like your asshole
every word I say is going into your asshole
and every word you say from now on
is your asshole talking through you
that new: job, book contract, lover
    awaits you
      you lucky assholes

AFTER A DEEP SLEEP I start to pick up the loose threads of the last few months. I go to the loft early in the morning. It is quiet. Sunlight is streaming into the living room through the eastern windows. The bookshelves. The white leather couches. The colorful shrine holding a bronze Buddha and a picture cut from a newspaper of a young boxer with a rippling six-pack. All glow in a static state caught between one world and the next.

Peter has slept. He is out. I am worried about his unpredictable behavior. He still has the old 12th Street apartment. He leaves his windows open for pigeons to enter. Feeds them on his bed. He overfills the bathtub. I can't manage Peter's behavior in the loft. I call Andrew Wylie (who is now co-executor with me) to ask him if I should change the locks to keep Peter out. He emphatically replies that I should.

The first memorial event is held at the small Jewel Heart Buddhist Center in a downtown Manhattan storefront. Allen's coffin is brought to the Center. Gelek Rinpoche presides over the service. Philip Glass and many sangha members are present. I read Allen's song-like poem *Gone, Gone, Gone.* Preface it by saying that I had not heard Allen read it. I am unsure if this is how he would read it. Then I read the poem. It feels like Allen is reading the poem through me. The rhythm takes over gone gone gone. It is like the slow ringing of a funeral bell. I seem to step out of my body. I hear my new voice for the first time but think it is Allen's voice. When I finish Philip Glass tells me. "That is exactly how he reads it." After the service we all go to a supper of momos (Tibetan for soup dumplings) at Joe's Shanghai restaurant on Pell Street. Rinpoche gets us all into the crowded Chinatown landmark but accidently leaves Bill Morgan off the list. When I notice that Bill is not at the table I run out to Pell Street but Bill is gone home.

———

The funeral plans are complicated. Allen is placed in an orthodox plain pine casket fastened with wooden pegs: no nails. Jews must get into the ground quickly to start feeding what Allen likes to call the *worm farm*. Buddhists cremate the plain coffin; there is no need for nails in the cremains.

———

Later I call Bill; yes, Bill is annoyed. It confirms Bill's suspicions of Buddhism. I worry about Bill as a distraction from my fears for future.

After the chanting, there are short speeches. Amiri Baraka speaks, Anne Waldman speaks, Peter Orlovsky speaks fairly lucidly, and I give unprepared remarks. *The Daily Forward* notes that I say that Allen somehow makes me Jewish.

This is Bob speaking at Allen's funeral. He looks composed and his spine is relatively straight. Head and neck are slightly forward as most readers and writers do. He is alone before the large group. Even his thoughts have abandoned him. He holds a plastic cup of water as if it is an unfathomable ocean. He is standing on the shore watching waves glitter in a sparkling play of ever changing colors. All thoughts vanish as he sees the end of infinity, as he always knew he would one day.

The next day is the large public funeral at the Shambhala Center. Gelek Rinpoche will preside again. Allen is there in his coffin. It is shrouded with white gauze and swathes of Buddhist primary colors. Rinpoche and the monks chant for a long spell. Hipsters. Beatniks. Social activists. Painters. Buddhists. Poets. Jews. Family. Press. The large assemblage shifts uncomfortably as the chanting drones on. There is faint odor of incense wafting over our heads. A soft rustling of stiff legs stretching to sit still for meditation is heard. Bill Morgan is at the side with my sons. They giggle each time Rinpoche chants Allen's name in his Tibetan accent. It sounds like "Gins a burger."

After a few more chants and several Poet Eulogies a large group of Jews emerges from the crowd. Circle Allen's coffin to chant the mourner's Kaddish. Allen's coffin is loaded into the hearse. Several of us watch him pull away from the curb. Rushing off on his way to his next destination.

Suddenly life settles down to a quiet routine. The very first thing I notice is that the phones stop ringing. After two decades of ceaseless telephone calls the silence is palpable. I have to face the truth that once again I am in a position of not knowing what I should do with myself. Allen's estate needs a lot of work. I will be very busy but I also know that my service to Allen is almost complete.

I am done with my journeyman years. I am now working for Allen Ginsberg the pure persona without the breathing Irwin within. But there are also the physical remains to settle. When Peter Hale and I receive Allen's ashes we pull out half the amount for Allen's family plot. This portion goes into the Ginsberg Litsky section of B'nai Israel Cemetery Newark. Under the big Budweiser sign by the airport. Louie is here. Edith will come. Rose is here. Joel will come here. Joel even poses for pictures prone on his grass spot. I ask the stone maker who now owns the cemetery if I can bury ashes. He tells me he doesn't care what I put in there as long as he makes the stone. Jews are not supposed to cremate so there is not much guidance here. I think about putting the ash into a cardboard shoebox as it will dissolve quickly. I remember that Rabbi Zalmon Shacter-Shalomi gives Allen a rainbow tallit (prayer shawl). I call him to ask if I can bury the tallit with Allen's cremains. Zalmon emphatically demands. "You will bury Allen **in** the tallit!" Ah thank God A Rabbi! "OK," I say. "Yes and cut off one of the tzitzit." "Oh why?" "You don't do mitzvot in the grave. And say Kaddish!" "I might not have a minyan." "Say Kaddish!!!" "OK will do!" Without much ado. We bury Allen's ashes wrapped in a colorful tallit tied up with Buddhist ribbons. It resembles a pretty football. I say Kaddish. We plan a stone dedication the next year. Edith comes. She is shocked that Allen is buried in her spot next to Louie. She will go in the plot next to Allen. "Oh Edith! Allen always wants to lie in your bed between you and Louie." She softens and smiles.

We divide the remainder of the cremains between Shambhala and Jewel Heart. Gelek Rinpoche tells us to put some of the ashes into the ocean. Peter and I launch some Allen ash off Coney Island pier. We include a macaroon for Allen to eat on his voyage. The cookie bobs along and allows us to track Allen on his low tide. Shambhala puts Allen's ashes and later Peter Orlovsky's into the foundation of a high altitude writing meditation shelter. This wind blown peak is at the **Shambhala Mountain Center near Red Feather Lakes Colorado.** Jewel Heart cryptically mixes Allen with other cremains of deep meditators. Steven Bornstein an old friend of Allen's suggests that I save some to place on the Mount of Olives in Jerusalem.

Peter Hale and I want to create living reminders of Allen on the Lower East Side. We plant a tree in Tompkins Square. There are protests at the planting because the erstwhile Lower East Side radicals believe that the Parks Department is co-opting the good name of Ginsberg. Less controversial and more poetic is the planting we install in the angle of the black iron 11th Street fence of St Mark's Churchyard. We settle on a kousa dogwood for it will bloom around Allen's birthday. The 3rd of June. The bush can be seen from anywhere on the street corner. It bends slightly to the east as if bowing in Bodhisattva humbleness to its beloved Lower East Side.

Which I do.

————

Along the East 11th Street fence is a series of modest trees; all planted for poets. Ed Sanders dubs it "Poets' Grove."

Kousa Dogwood in St. Mark's Yard on Allen's birthday June 3. Photo by Bob.

Allen uses an old lawyer friend who decades before helped him obtain copies of his personal governmental papers through The Freedom of Information Act. Apparently the lawyer has lost his acumen since. Allen creates a Living Trust to avoid losing control of the estate in probate, and to reduce estate taxes. The language of the trust says that Allen, "*should* make charitable contributions." However, *Estate Law For Dummies* makes it clear that the document has to read, "***must*** make contributions" in order to take advantage of the tax deduction. This one word error costs the estate roughly a total of $300,000 in taxes.

Allen's teachers' union helps us move his pension fund into the Living Trust. However, no one reminds us that we need to also move the *death benefit* into the trust. This document determines where Allen's pension funds will go in case he predeceases his retirement. The death benefit gives the assets directly to Peter Orlovsky. Allen is not yet retired at the time of his death; Peter is to inherit about $180,000.

A rude shock comes when I show Allen's estate to our new legal team. They are horrified at the inept legal handling of Allen's affairs.

Allen does not have cash assets except for his copyrights and pension from Brooklyn College. The physical property is his loft.

Archives amassed since the Stanford sale. Personal possessions including many signed pieces of art.

Money is necessary but always a nuisance to Allen. He cannot imagine his life boiling down to some numbers. He doesn't want to hurt anyone with the money in the estate. He wants to protect me from Peter. Allen needs to protect Peter from Peter's self-destructive habits.

Peter is still using hard drugs. Handing him a large amount of money definitely endangers his safety. Peter likes to carry a fat wad of bills when he hits the streets high on crack. Peter is as displaced in his world as I am in mine. He struggles to assert his rights. For the first time he calls himself Mrs. Allen Ginsberg.

The delicacy of distributing money to Peter concerns both Peter and me. It is true that I am not reconciled with Peter. It is also true I fear for his life. Friends spot him screaming staggering in the middle of rush hour Sixth Avenue traffic. I call for advice among Allen's oldest sangha friends. These officers of Shambhala were close to Trungpa Rinpoche. Charles and Judy Lief emerge as the people to help Peter in his time of great need. Peter adores Judy. She is Peter's meditation instructor. Charles practices law. Hopefully he can arrange a new trust to protect Peter.

Judy talks to Peter. Charles and Peter's lawyer create a will and a trust for Peter. Now that the trust exists I stop stalling about distributing the funds.

October 7 1999 is the date of our estate sale. There are a lot of unforeseen taxes to pay. We want to make a distribution to the heirs. Allen's material possessions have to be sold off. These items are not a part of the archives at Stanford University. Paintings. Clothing. Pens. Shrine objects. Cameras. Ephemera. Memo-

———

Allen does not want to add harm to Peter and adamantly wants his financial legacy to be distributed through a third party.

———

Peter is visiting one and all and smearing my name. He whispers that I stole the loft from him, that I stole his money, and that I stole his farm in upstate New York. There is nothing I can do to reestablish my good name without violating Peter's privacy and Allen's desire not to hurt. My prayers include a plea for help to *ignore those who slander me.*

———

I contact a downtown lawyer that had worked for Peter several years ago when Allen and Peter draw up a legal separation agreement.

I appraise the new lawyer of the need to form a trust to manage all the money from Brooklyn College.

Andy Clausen visits me and complains to me about my treatment of Peter. Because it is happily settled, I tell Andy what has happened and why. He gets it and sees why it is best for me to stay quiet until this time.

The Inspector has a personal interest in Ginsberg and wants to see the objects. I pull the most interesting (and least valuable) possessions into the foreground of the pile. The inspector is shown into Edith's room and I tell stories about the things within easy reach.

On the day after the auction materials are picked up, Larry Rivers' plumber leaves a faucet running. Edith's room is flooded. There is a lot of ceiling & wall damage; the cost to Larry could easily have been several hundred thousand dollars of Allen's household.

The catalog for the auction provides an intimate way to view Allen's life as solely defined by the objects he chooses to surround himself with.

Stanford already owns Allen's personal library, which is why Peter crazily forces people to steal Allen's books during the wake. We collect them from the unwilling thieves later. One thief who can't break old habits is Gregory Corso. He steals Allen's copy of *Mindfield*, Corso's own poetry, which is heavily annotated in Allen's hand. Maybe Gregory gets good dollars for it, but really he denies future scholars insights into his poetry.

rabilia. All of these items are stacked in Edith's room. Our estate lawyers assure me that the IRS will never come to inspect the items in person. This time they do.

I entertain the IRS officer with stories about Allen's possessions. He is satisfied after an hour. The next day all the Ginsberg objects are picked up by Sotheby's.

Bill Morgan organizes the auction. He and I give tours to people before the auction date. There is a special performance to mark the occasion. Ed Sanders performs his lament for Allen. Paul Simon sings Allen's *Father Death Blues*. The most amazing artifact at the auction is Allen's original harmonium with its black case covered in stickers from around the world. The filmmaker Obie Benz buys it. The bidding is high for Allen's Montblanc pen. You can now find it at the Montblanc Museum in France. Goldie Hawn's daughter buys several of the shrine items for her mother. The auction is successful for the Ginsberg Trust. Allen's celebrity is treated with proper pomp and real respect. We pay out all the earnings.

We prepare the last ten years of Allen's literary achievements for a second sale to Stanford. We get a new appraisal. Allen's worth increases after his death. The final ten years are worth more than the first forty combined. We are loath to break the collection up. If we had the correct language in the trust document we can receive a tax deduction for the amount we donate. The value above the sale price would be large. This is where the mistake regarding making donations hampers us. Because I now have fiscal responsibility I cannot seem to sell the archives below its assessment. We must set a price for the sale at the valuation that Stanford can financially manage. We do not gain any tax advantage to offset other income taxes. However Allen's archives are complete at Stanford.

Peter's landlord sees an opportunity to take back the East 12th Street apartments. He sues Peter. He sues me too because in the past I sign the rent checks for Allen. At the same time Charles is attempting to be named Peter's legal guardian. The judge on the landlord's case recognizes Peter name. Even knows his poetry. She takes over the guardianship case. Combines it with the landlord case. The judge is worried about me cheating Peter. She attempts to force Andrew and me to make the Trust documents public. We are not legally obligated to do. I am worried about having to expose all this *sensitive bullshit* in public. I don't like Peter but I respect Allen's love for him. Peter apologizes to me on several occasions but his apologies are lacking in conviction. How can Peter ever actually compensate me for the harm his threats to my children causes?

The judge convenes a hearing in court that I am not privy to. She calls Peter in to depose him on my actions. The judge leads Peter through many questions designed to prompt him to complain about me. Peter refuses. In fact Peter praises me highly. Makes no complaints. Later after hearing of this I can take my first step toward restoring Peter to my good graces. I no longer consider him dead. Peter likes to act with contrariness to authority. This might explain his testimony. I prefer to think that Peter tells the truth in a courtroom because he realizes that I am truly trying to help him by honoring Allen's intentions.

Peter does come under the guardianship of Charles Lief. He stays in the apartment until new arrangements are made. This entire process takes almost two years. Allen's legacy to Peter is sufficient to allow him to live in supervised housing in New England. It is very near Karma Chöling. This is Peter's favorite Buddhist center. I often hear Peter in deep psychotic intoxication wail out. "I want to be chained to a monastery wall!" Peter now enjoys more than ten years amid a caring Buddhist community. This is his longest adult period of sobriety. He still cycles through various psychic stages but these are less extreme and more manageable. Peter dies peacefully on May 30, 2010.

There are a group of prayers in Judaism called Yizkor prayers. They are prayers to recall former loved ones. We praise God in order to recall the positive accomplishments of the departed. In one sense saying the mourner's Kaddish is carrying the goodness of the non-living further in life. The years after Allen's death are filled with Yizkor work for Peter Hale and me. We have books to publish. Last poems. Selected essays. Selected interviews. These three books are on Allen's mind before he dies. Allen's last poem "Things I'll Not Do (Nostalgias)" is the only typescript that Allen does not get to proofread at least once. Peter Hale and I pour over the poem to transcribe its difficult scrawl. Many people help us. There is one phrase that none of us are sure about. We have to drop that line. The poem remains incomplete at the close of *Death and Fame*.

Allen's last poems are both simple and complex. Some are schoolyard rhymes that have contiguous themes and rhythms. They are masterfully crafted. Allen's liver is failing. He is slightly addled. During his last hospital stay he thinks about nursery rhymes. He asks me to recite from memory the poem about the little piggies. "This little piggy went to market . . ." When I reach

———

Although I do not visit Peter in his sober years, I always keep informed on how he is faring. He calls me once to tell me that he has found a trunk full of unpublished Ginsberg poems. I say that I am excited to hear that. He tells me that Allen had left instructions with him to have them published. Peter sounds like he is very manic. I calmly tell Peter that this is great news and ask him to send me a couple of the poems so I can get started working on it right away. Then he tells me that Pete Seeger and Bob Dylan are on the way over to see him. I ask him to extend my warm regards to these illustrious guests. I wish him well, and I actually keep one eye out for these poems to arrive!

———

Can Allen have been predicting this very community in the first part of *Howl*? Fourteen years after his death, the advent of the internet leads Peter Hale to solve Allen's strophic intent. The illegible words quickly come up correct in Wikipedia. The completed poem can be found at my middle finger "this little piggy had roast beef." Allen cries out "Ah ha! Something is wrong! That line is changed somewhere. Pigs don't eat meat!" I am pretty sure that they do eat meat but I don't contradict Allen. He brilliantly rewrites the line to read "This little piggy ate quiche." Allen requests my sons' old copy of Rackham's *Mother Goose*. He pores through it searching for more understanding. Just days before his end Allen finds brilliance in the very early morning sky. Stars show him the compass of his life. The dialogue with these stars is his *Starry Rhymes*.

Without Allen I lose a quarter of my income. It is generated from my agenting fees from Allen's paid appearances. I need to make up that income. It occurs to me that I can teach. So at a Kiddush (blessed) lunch after services Gail brashly asks me "So what are you going to do now that your boss is dead?" "I don't know – teach?" I stammer. "Wait." she says. Brings her lover Pat over. Pat teaches English at City Tech CUNY in Brooklyn. She urgently needs a replacement adjunct. I start teaching part-time.

After we publish the three planned posthumous books - *Death and Fame. Deliberate Prose. Spontaneous Minds* - I start to feel the slowdown of work in the office. Peter Hale oversees the creation of a website for Allen. Allen does not want to be made into a museum. A website is an active teaching tool. *Allenginsberg.org* is content-rich. It receives large surges of use at the end of each academic term as papers come due. We hope there might yet be a Ginsberg curriculum at a university. Poetry. Buddhism. Photography. Blues. Social justice. Freedom of speech. Song writing. How to repair a world stricken with AIDS-like global degradation. These concentrations would make well-rounded citizens out of students.

www.*allenginsberg.org*.

————

I realize that I really enjoy teaching and soon understand that teaching is the closest thing to working with Allen. It engages deep communication with personal trust and integrity. Working with Allen puts me into a maelstrom of information, social actions, artistic expression, selfless lobbying, and sharing of information. Teaching is a similar set of tasks to juggle. I feel connected and useful again.

————

Allen doesn't have enough time to give Peter Hale and me guidance as to how best carry on his legacy. He makes one definite statement, "Do not make a museum out of me!" This means that we should not make his loft into a shrine or a center in his name. I collect many little odds and ends from Allen's life such as pens, eyeglasses, small awards, coins from travels, roach clips, his "works", a William Burroughs empty methadone bottle etc. When Allen leaves 12th Street, I throw it all into an empty red toolbox. This is the Allen Ginsberg museum!

———

There is no longer enough work for two of us. I am depressed with my sinecure. I start to think that I should move on. I wonder whether working so long with Allen is harmful to the writer in me. At Allen's

death, I realize that it is good for me to have completed my apprenticeship with Allen. I find that I have a new voice and acuity in communication. Something from Allen rubs off on me.

———

The Pequod is Allen's body. It carries all the players and attracts the white whale of Poetry. Ishmael alone survives; this is us.

———

Allen is pleased that I would write about our work. In one of our last conversations, he asks me if it would be like *Cleaning Up New York* (my 1976 book on cleaning houses). I say, "Yes. I will try to be funny and useful." He smiles and squeezes my hand.

Very soon after Allen's death I am stripping the hospital bed that Allen dies in. It is to be picked up later that day by Hospice. I put my right hand and bare forearm under the mattress to pull the edge of the sheet out. My hand and arm are instantly coated with a thick wet slime. This is Allen's body fluid that drained through the mattress during his long Samadhi in death. I yank my arm out. Hold it up. Stare at my glistening hand and forearm with part horror and wonder. Allen's Bodhisattva soaks into my hand and arm. I run to the sink to wash it off. Later that day I talk to Rinpoche's secretary Kathy Laretz. I mention this slimy experience to her. She calls back to tell me that Rinpoche tells her that this is significant.

I work for Allen for twenty years of his lifetime and then ten more Yizkor years. I always have just the *beginnings of ambition.* Thus I always need challenge in life to remain the perpetual beginner. I decide to apply for a full-time teaching job. Working for a private Jewish high school would both fit my interests and broaden my participation in Jewish practice. Allen's father Louis had been a Paterson High School English teacher. Allen starts to wear a coat and tie after Louis's death. I too leave the Ginsberg world. Put on a second-hand coat and tie to teach high school English.

My new practice faces young Bodhisattvas in their seats. I teach them how to read their own physical reactions to literature. I delineate how to use analytical arguments based on these responses to fashion original criticism. Allen helps me refine these methods for myself. People now think of me as writing poetry in a Ginsbergian style. The truth is that my poems are straight around Allen.

Photo by Isaac Rosenthal

Acknowledgements

This book is dedicated to the many lives of Irwin Allen Ginsberg.

This narrative is edited by E. Claman. A muse of profound clarity. In a tabloid flurry, E. nightly ferried marked-up pages to me. I worked at dawn to address E.'s emendations and promptings for new writing. If it makes any sense to you, it is because of Claman's sure navigation.

Thank you to friends and family who read early drafts of *Straight Around Allen* manuscript and offered sage advise: Rochelle Kraut, David S. Wills, Eliot Katz, Jeffrey Posternak, Ellie Wiesenfeld, Henry Condell, Simon Schuchat, Bill Morgan, Philip Turner, Simon Pettet, Isaac Rosenthal, Sandra Silverman, Michael McClure, and Michael Schumacher. A special thanks is due Peter Hale who has aided this volume in a myriad of ways.

Writings and photography by Allen Ginsberg are used by permission of Allen Ginsberg LLC.

Photographs by Brian Graham are used by permission.

Photographs by Isaac Rosenthal are used by permission

Photograph by Fred McDarrah is used by permission of McDarrah estate:

> Poet, Beat Generation figure and cultural icon Allen Ginsberg with a paper hat decorated with stars and stripes sits on the Central Park bandstand at rally at conclusion of 5th Avenue Peace Demonstration to Stop the War in Vietnam, New York, New York, March 26, 1966

36904540R00107

Made in the USA
Columbia, SC
28 November 2018